CW00395138

The
Murder
Almanac

Richard and Molly
Whittington-Egan

Neil Wilson Publishing • Glasgow

Published by Neil WIlson Publishing Ltd
11 West Chapelton Crescent, Glasgow G61 2DE.

A catalogue record for this book is available from the
British Library.

ISBN 1-897784-04-X

Typeset in 9pt on 10pt Baskerville by Origination, and
printed by Scotprint Ltd in Musselburgh.

Acknowledgments

Clearly, in an extended compilatory work of this kind we are indebted to friends and fellow-tillers of many areas of the criminous field for a share in their hard-won croppings.

We wish to acknowledge and thank them.

Jonathan Goodman, comrade in arms through many struggles.

Donald Rumbelow and Robin Odell, old friends and pioneer labourers in the killing fields of Jack the Ripper. Paul Begg, Martin Fido, and Keith Skinner, young friends and leaders of the new wave of Ripper experts. Also that determinedly debunking sole practitioner and good companion, Melvin Harris.

Across the water . . .

Albert Borowitz, who can always be relied upon for ungrudging help with problems of transatlantic malfeasance. Clinton Krauss, one of the most tenacious – and generous – of bibliophiles, whose bibliotechnic assistance and splendid contribution of friendship – and rare volumes – are much prized by us. And Robert A. Flynn, of Portland, Maine, stalwart support and positive encyclopaedist of all matters concerning the late Miss Lizbeth Borden, of Fall River.

Finally, an indispensable quartet of Universal Providers of totally unobtainable works – Camille Wolff of London; The Elmers – Clifford and Marie – of Cheadle Hulme; Patterson Smith of New Jersey; and Jack Bradstreet of Melbourne.

RICHARD AND MOLLY WHITTINGTON – EGAN

The Silencers of the Lambs

The old order of murder is changing. The cosy domestic poisonings of Victorian, Edwardian and Georgian England, the almost jaunty blood-lettings with knife, gun and blunt instrument, the tidier ligatures with rope, cord and thin-biting wire, all these purposive acts, motivated by comprehensible, if not excusable, human passions of love and malice, greed and gain, of the first three-quarters of our century, have been overshadowed by the emergence of the terrifying Silencer of the Lambs. He is the random repeat killer, slaying total strangers for the sheer recreational love of killing. He is the Serial Killer.

The name was coined, so the story goes, in the 1970s, by FBI agent, Robert K. Ressler, for the engagingly down-to-earth reason that such multiple murderers, killing in series as they do, reminded him of the cliffhanger film serials that he watched at the Saturday morning cinema in his home-town as a child.

But what exactly *is* a serial killer? How does he differ from a mass murderer? Is it simply a matter of semantics? Both, surely, are multiple murderers. The determining diagnostic feature has to be the psychological motivation of the killer. The mass murderer kills numbers of people for any one, or any combination of, the classic motives – gain, revenge, elimination, jealousy, conviction, which is to say killing for an idea or ideal. The serial killer kills primarily for a compulsive sexual reason, or for pure love and lust for killing; although, of course, just to make things more complicated, incidental benefits may accrue to be taken advantage of.

The serial killer is not a new species of homicidal monster. It is just that, like the dinosaurs in Jurassic times, he has increased and multiplied to crescendo proportions since the 1980s. Serial murder is a growth industry. The up-and-coming thing. Years of rapt experimentation and innovation lie ahead.

The serial killer concept may be an American invention, but one of the earliest of the breed was British – Jack the Ripper. Other British examples are Christie the Notting Hill Necrophile, Brady and Hindley the Moors Murderers, Peter Sutcliffe the Yorkshire Ripper, and Dennis Nilsen. Undeniably, though, it is America that has yielded the thickest crop. Seventy-five per cent of known cases of serial killing have occurred in the United States. This must, however, be balanced against the fact that the most sophisticated, high-tech, state-of-the-art serial killer tracking techniques are also American.

The in-depth study of the serial killer by behavioural analysis has been undertaken by a crack team of FBI specialists, the Behavioural Science Unit (BSU), at the FBI Academy, which stands, stoutly fenced and defended of access, in 600 acres of woodland at Quantico, Virginia.

The Quantico behaviouralists have put together the typical profile of the serial killer: most are solitary males, although some hunt in pairs. About eight per cent are females: nurses or baby-sitters who kill their charges, wives and mistresses who murder a series of husbands or lovers. About ten per cent are doctors, dentists or professional health workers. Almost a third are former mental patients or ex-convicts. They come from all walks of life and are frequently the products of broken or severely brutal homes and have been subjected to cruelty, sexual abuse, and even torture, in deprived childhood. Quite often they have suffered head injuries. Early symptoms characteristically displayed include bed-wetting (after the age of twelve), fire-raising and sadism towards animals. They routinely graduate to thievery. Later, fear and distrust of women may be manifest. Part of the pattern, too, are alcohol and drug abuse, plus pornography, as buttresses for their high dominance requirements and aids to escape into a comfortable realm of fantasising. Returning to the scene of the crime is a not uncommon behavioural feature. The clues they leave behind are little more than semen and pubic hairs. Interestingly in this context, the British serial killer, John Francis Duffy, aged 30, the so-called Railway Rapist, whose sexual assaults escalated to murder in 1985-6, having perhaps heard of the recent forensic advance of genetic fingerprinting, or possibly aware of the fact that blood group identification could be made from sperm, stuffed burning paper handkerchief tissues into the victim's genitals in order to destroy sperm traces from which the distinctive pattern of the DNA in his body cells could be identified. Serial killings are usually intraracial.

A product of the BSU is the National Center for the Analysis of Violent Crime (NCAVC), set up in 1984 in a huge, windowless, concrete bunker sixty feet below the Academy. America is so vast, not to say complex, with some 16,855 separate police, sheriff and law enforcement agencies, that the transient, itinerant or journeyman murderer poses a desperately difficult hunting prospect. A serial killer trolling for victims can cross any number of state lines and commit his crimes in any number of different jurisdictions, between which there will be no communication or, worse, the deliberate silence of jealous territorialism. Thus, the co-ordinating of geographically, and geopolitically, spread data is the vital function contribution by the NCAVC, where every murder committed in the United States is registered and analysed on computer, and whose central data pool is available to all law enforcement bodies. It is at once a clearing house and a resource centre in the national fight against the menace of the footloose violent criminal.

The steady and perturbing upsurge of the dreadful Silencer of the Lambs is attested to by the fact that nearly half of our 101 murderers turn out to be serial killers. Happily, though, they have not managed to burke entirely the old, gentle pioneers like Major Armstrong, Drs. Crippen, Cream, Pritchard and Ruxton, Mesdames Bartlett, Bravo, Maybrick, Kent and Smith, or such enduring partnerships as those of Messrs. Burke and Hare and Bywaters and Thompson. Neither have the great enigmas, Oscar Slater and Herbert William Wallace been elbowed out by those who have elected, in some instances, for quantity rather than quality.

The international brotherhood of people who know about real-life crime carry within their heads, like so many masonic signs, certain emblems of the Great Ones . . . The "scuse fingers!' of the Armstrong case. The held big toe of the Bartlett case. The 'Hot water! Hot water!' of the Bravo case. The terrible breakfast of the Borden case. The cyclops eye of the Ruxton case. 'Qualtrough' on the telephone in the Wallace case. They will, perhaps, find also here, among the latest cropping of memorables, some new seductive tesserae to add to their personal mosaics.

RICHARD AND MOLLY WHITTINGTON-EGAN

Major Herbert Rowse Armstrong

The Hay Poisoner

Murderer: Major Herbert Rowse Armstrong.
Victim: Katharine Mary Armstrong (48): wife.
Locus: Mayfield, Cusop, Hay, Breconshire, Wales.
Date: February 22nd, 1921.
Means: Slow poisoning with arsenic.
Motive: Elimination of burdensome wife; amatory freedom; financial gain.
Crimewatch: Born in Plymouth, May 13th, 1869. Went up to Cambridge. Qualified as a solicitor. Practised in Liverpool, Newton Abbot and, finally, Hay. Supporting the twin afflictions of doses of syphilis and a nagging wife, turned to salvarsan and arsenic as life-enhancers. Plagued also by dandelions, proclaiming his determination to be rid of pests, the little Major went to war, openly, against the dandelions, and, secretly, against Mrs. Armstrong, armed with the 'magic bullets'. These foes vanquished, he then conducted a losing campaign against his rival solicitor, Oswald Martin, to whom at afternoon tea one day he handed an arsenic-loaded scone with the immortal words, "'scuse fingers!' These modest essays into self-betterment sadly misfired, with the result that the enterprising little man who strutted around Hay wearing riding boots, breeches, British warm and his wartime majority, became the only solicitor to be hanged – on May 31st, 1922 – for murder. And the dandelions of Cusop increased and multiplied.

Prime sources: *Notable British Trial,* edited by Filson Young, William Hodge, Edinburgh, 1927.
Murder Revisited, John Rowland, John Long, London, 1961.
Exhumation of a Murder, Robin Odell, Harrap, London, 1975.

Jeremy Bamber

Murderer: Jeremy Bamber.
Victims: Neville Bamber (61): adoptive father. June Bamber (61): adoptive mother. Sheila Caffell (27): adoptive sister. Daniel Caffell and Nicholas Caffell, her six-year-old twins.
Locus: White House Farm, Pages Lane, Tolleshunt D'Arcy, Essex.
Date: August 7th, 1985.
Means: Shooting with a .22 Anschutz semi-automatic rifle.
Motive: Gain: to inherit a £400,000 family fortune.
Crimewatch: Coldly planned massacre for cold cash. Born in 1961, the illegitimate child of a vicar's daughter, Bamber was adopted by a well-to-do farming family. Sent to boarding-school, he saw it as rejection, and turned against his adoptive parents. In his twenties his taste ran to Porsches and free-spending sprees. To finance the good life, he decided to accelerate his inheritance by killing off the family – making it look as if his sister, who had suffered mental illness, had gone berserk with a gun and then committed suicide. He attended the mass funeral in a designer suit, £30 tie and wearing white make-up to look more drawn. His mistress, Julie Mugford, who said he strangled rats with his bare hands to test his resolve, gave evidence against him. He was sentenced at Chelmsford to five concurrent life sentences.

Prime source: *Contemporary newspapers.*

Velma (Margie) Barfield

Mass murderer

Murderer: Velma (Margie) Barfield.
Victims: Convicted of the murder of Stuart Taylor (56): fiancé. Admitted in court, after conviction, during sentencing phase, to murder of: Lillie Bullard (64): her own mother. Dolly Edwards (85): Stuart Taylor's aunt and Velma Barfield's patient. John Henry Lee (81): husband of one of Velma Barfield's patients..
Locus: North Carolina.
Dates: December 30th, 1974 (Bullard). March 1st, 1977 (Edwards). June 4th, 1977 (Lee). February 3rd, 1978 (Taylor).
Means: Arsenic: ant poison (Lee and Taylor); rat poison (Bullard and Edwards).
Motive: Curious. Money, according to due process of law, was at the root of it all. She killed Mother to conceal the fact that she had borrowed $1,000 from a money-lender, who was pressing, having put up her mother's effects as collateral and used her Social Security card as identification. As for Stuart Taylor, she had forged his signature on three moderate cheques. No known motive for the other murders.
Crimewatch: Velma Barfield was a nurse, thought of as an angel of mercy, and a grandmother. She overreached herself with her last victim, Stuart Taylor, who died, not at home, but in hospital, with no apparent cause of death. Arsenic was found in the liver. The body of Velma Barfield's second husband, Jennings Barfield, who had died in 1970, was also found, on exhumation, to contain arsenic, but that case was not proceeded with. John Henry Lee's invalid wife was still alive. Traces of arsenic were

found in her living hair, but that case, too, was not proceeded with. A defence of insanity by reason of a ten-year dependence on Valium failed. In prison, Velma Barfield became a born-again Christian. Her last meal on Death Row was fried chicken livers, macaroni and cheese, collard greens, beans, bread, cake with peanut-butter icing and an iced drink. On November 2nd, 1984, aged 52, Velma Barfield, dressed in pink pyjamas, was executed in Raleigh by lethal injection of procuronium bromide, a muscle relaxant.

Prime source: *Contemporary newspapers.*

Adelaide Blanche Bartlett

The Pimlico Mystery

Accused: Adelaide Blanche Bartlett.
Victim: Thomas Edwin Bartlett (41): husband.
Locus: 85 Claverton Street, Pimlico, London.
Date: January 1st, 1886.
Means: Chloroform by mouth.
Motive: Elimination of unwanted husband.
Crimewatch: Adelaide, certifiedly the daughter of Adolphe Collet de la Tremoille, Comte de Thouars d'Escury, allegedly the natural daughter of an undeclaring Englishman of great wealth and even greater consequence, born in Orleans on December 19th, 1855, married, under conditions to say the least bizarre, a humble, but aspiring, young grocer, Thomas Edwin Bartlett. The couple lived above the shop at Herne Hill, before transferring, via Merton Abbey, to Pimlico. Along the way they became entangled with a distinctly odd, 27-year-old Wesleyan cleric, the Reverend George Dyson, to whom Bartlett 'gave' his wife in the event of his demise, and who, impatient it seems, 'took' her prior to that sad occasion, in consequence whereof George and Adelaide found themselves in the dock. Her reverend companion, procurer of chloroform by appointment, having been pronounced an innocent, it still required all the forensic skill of Sir Edward Clarke to negotiate her acquittal. Whispers of Adelaide's noble birth confused the issue, as did the erroneous notion of liquid chloroform as an excruciatingly painful, impossibly difficult to administer, substance. Sir James Paget, Sergeant-Surgeon to the Queen, remarked that now that she had been found not guilty, Mrs. Bartlett 'should tell us in the interests of science how she did it.'

Prime sources: *The Trial of Adelaide Bartlett for Murder,* edited by Edward Beal, Stevens & Haynes, London, 1886.
Notable British Trial, edited by Sir John Hall, William Hodge, Edinburgh, 1927.
Did Adelaide Bartlett . . . ? Gordon Gwynn, Christopher Johnson, London, 1950.
Poison and Adelaide Bartlett, Yseult Bridges, Hutchinson, London, 1962.
Second edition, Macmillan, London, 1970.
The Pimlico Murder, Kate Clarke, Souvenir Press, London, 1990.

Robert Berdella

Serial killer

Murderer: Robert Berdella.
Victims: Larry Wayne Pearson (21). Gerald Howell (20). Robert Sheldon (18). Mark Wallace (20). Walter Ferris (20). Todd Stoops.
Locus: House on Charlotte Street, Hyde Park, Kansas City, Missouri.
Dates: 1984-7.
Means: Raped and tortured to death – hung upside down, electric shocks, suffocated with plastic bag.
Motive: Homosexual sadistic slayings.
Crimewatch: Berdella (born 1949), calling-card, "I rise from death. I kill death, and death kills me. Although I carry poison in my head the antidote can be found in my tail, which I bite with rage," owned Bob's Bizarre Bazaar, an occult curio shop. On April 2nd, 1988, a neighbour found a naked youth, Christopher Bryson, shivering at her front door. He was purple with welts and bruises, and he was wearing a dog's collar. After four days of torture, with Berdella injecting him in the throat, saying that the substance was a drain cleaner, Bryson had escaped by burning through his ropes with a book of matches. Police found some 200 Polaroid snapshots of rape, torture and death. Robert Sheldon's head was dug up from the garden. Larry Pearson's jawbone was also unearthed. On August 3rd, 1988, Berdella pleaded guilty to the murder of Pearson and was sentenced to life imprisonment. On December 20th, 1988, he confessed to five more murders and was sentenced to five concurrent life terms.

Prime source: *Contemporary newspapers.*

David Richard Berkowitz alias Son of Sam

Serial killer

Murderer: David Richard Berkowitz alias Son of Sam.
Victims: Donna Lauria (18). Christine Freund (26).
Virginia Voskerichian (19). Valentina Suriani (18).
Alexander Esau (20). Stacy Moskowitz (20).
Locus: New York: Brooklyn, the Bronx and Queens.
Dates: July 1976 – July 1977.
Means: Shooting by .44-calibre Bulldog revolver.
Motive: No rational motive. Berkowitz preyed on
courting couples in parked cars, impelled by
'demons' in his mind, which commanded him to kill
young women – to 'conquer' them because he could
not seduce them.
Crimewatch: A genuine case of insane killing – no
question of feigned psychosis here – as evidenced by
his post-capture writings, and by the state of his lair at
35 Pine Street, Yonkers, where grey blankets blocked
out the windows and messages were scrawled on the
walls. Berkowitz, born in 1953, loner, arsonist, security
guard, was severely deluded and vividly hallucinated,
tormented by demon dogs. He was caught through a
traffic violation ticket. Glad that it was over, he
pleaded guilty and was sentenced to 365 years'
imprisonment.

Prime sources: *Son of Sam,* George Carpozi, Jr., Manor
Books, New York, 1977.
Son of Sam, Lawrence D. Klausner, McGraw-Hill, New York,
1981.
Confessions of Son of Sam, David Abrahamsen, Columbia
University Press, New York, 1985.
The Ultimate Evil, Maury Terry, Grafton Books, London,
1988.

Kenneth Alessio Bianchi

The Hillside Stranglers

Serial killers

Angelo Buono

Murderers: Kenneth Alessio Bianchi. Angelo Buono.
Victims: Elissa Teresa Kastin (21). Yolanda Washington (19) (Buono not convicted of this murder). Judith Lynn Miller (15). Kristina Weckler (20). Dolores Cepeda (12). Sonja Johnson (14). Jane Evelyn King (28). Lauren Rae Wagner (18). Kimberley Diane Martin (18). Cindy Lee Hudspeth (20). Committed by Bianchi only: Karen Mandic (22) and Diane Wilder (27).
Loci: Buono's home: 703 East Colorado Street, Glendale, Los Angeles – first ten murders except Yolanda Washington, who was killed in a car on the freeway. Catlows' House, Bayside Drive, Bellingham, Washington State – the last two murders.
Dates: October 1977 – February 1978 (First ten murders).
January 11th, 1979 (Last two killings).
Means: Strangulation with a ligature.
Motive: Sexual gratification: rape and torture.
Crimewatch: Cousins by blood, accomplices in atrocity, Bianchi (26) and Buono (44) splayed nude bodies of girls on hillsides roughly concentric to Buono's house. Removed to Bellingham on an adventure of his own, Bianchi was easily arrested by association with Karen Mandic, and the list of convictions flowed from that

point. To escape death penalty in Washington, Bianchi faked multiple personality. Then entered into a plea-bargaining deal whereby he pleaded guilty and testified against Buono in California. Both sentenced to life imprisonment.

Prime sources: *The Hillside Strangler,* Ted Schwarz, Doubleday, New York, 1981.
Two of a Kind, Darcy O'Brien, New American Library, New York, 1985.

Bible John

**True identity
unknown**

Serial killer

Murderer: Bible John.
Victims: Patricia Docker (25). Jemima ('Mima')
McDonald (32). Helen Puttock (29).
Loci: Naked in the door recess of a back lane lock-
up garage, Carmichael Lane, Battlefield, South
Glasgow (Docker). Partly clothed in a bed recess in a
derelict tenement at 23 Mackeith Street, Bridgeton,
Glasgow (McDonald). Fully clothed, lying against a
back-court wall of Earl Street, Scotstoun, Glasgow
(Puttock).
Dates: February 22nd-23rd, 1968 (Docker). August
16th-17th, 1969 (McDonald). October 30th-31st, 1969
(Puttock).
Means: Strangulation as with a belt or something
strong, and face and head injuries caused by kicking
and punching (Docker). Strangled with her own
tights (McDonald). Strangled with one of her
stockings. Bruising to the face. Clothes in disarray
(Puttock).
Motive: Sexual gratification – one way or another.
*Crimewatch:*The unholy John collected his partners
for the *danse macabre* that ended in a back-street
death, from the concrete palais known as the
Barrowland Ballroom. The notion is that his intention
was, if thwarted, rape. But there was no clear evidence
of sexual assault. Extraordinarily, all three victims
were menstruating. Described by Helen Puttock's
sister, Jeannie Williams, who met the man, as a
handsome six-footer, age 25-35, with beautifully
barbered, short-back-and-sides red hair, with a
quotation from the Good Book ever ready on his
tongue, he vanished like cigarette smoke. For the first

time in a Scottish murder hunt the Crown Office
allowed the publication of an artist's impression of a
man suspected of a serious crime. It was no use. The
dancing psychopath has never been found. Hope
surged in 1983. A man returned after ten years in
Australia recognised Bible John as a friend he used to
go to the dancing with at the Barrowland. Traced to a
village near Amsterdam, the friend proved a
remarkable look-alike, but there wasn't a scrap of
evidence to tie him to the Glasgow dance of death
killings. To this day wry memories linger in the tough
heart of Glasgow of the terrible coming of Bible John.

Prime source: *Bible John,* Charles N. Stoddart, Paul Harris
Publishing, Edinburgh, 1980.

Lawrence Sigmund (or Sigmond) Bittaker

Serial killer

Murderer: Lawrence Sigmund (or Sigmond) Bittaker.

Victims: Jacqueline Leah Lamp (13). Jackie Gilliam (15). Shirley Ledford (16). Lucinda Schaefer (16). Andrea Hall (18).

Loci: The suburbs of Los Angeles. Victims from Redondo Beach (Lamp, Gilliam), Sun Valley (Ledford), Torrance (Schaefer), Tujunga (Hall).

Dates: June to October, 1979.

Means: Strangling.

Motive: Sex and torture.

Crimewatch: Bittaker, a 40-year-old Burbank, California, machinist, teamed up with Roy Lewis Norris. The pair of sadists are said to have planned to kill one female victim of each teen age from 13 through to 19, inclusive, but were captured while still three victims short of completing their goal. Their method was to lure girl hitch-hikers into their van, nicknamed 'Murder Mac'. The girls would then be raped and tortured and mutilated, with pliers, an icepick and sledgehammer, before being strangled to death. They were charged on April 28th, 1980. Norris agreed to plead guilty to involvement in the murders on the understanding that the prosecutor would not ask for the death penalty. He received a sentence of 45 years to life. Bittaker, found guilty on February 17th, 1981, after California's first televised trial, was sentenced to death. He awaits execution in San Quentin.

Prime source: *Contemporary newspapers.*

The Black Dahlia – Elizabeth Short

Identity unknown

The Black Dahlia Murder

Murderer: Unknown.

Victim: Elizabeth Ann Short.

Locus: Vacant lot, South Norton Avenue, between 39th and Coliseum Streets, a block east of Crenshaw Boulevard, Los Angeles.

Date: January 15th, 1947.

Means: Choked to death on her own blood.

Motive: Sexual gratification – just possibly tinged with revenge.

Crimewatch: Indulgence of sadistic frenzy. Body drained of every drop of blood. Subjected to some very fancy knife-work, including the letters 'BD' cut into the flesh of the thigh. Elizabeth Short, a Hollywood drifter with stardom dust in her eyes, was the ideal victim. Nicknamed the Black Dahlia because of her alluring trademark of seductive black clothing, she had a chequered history of juvenile delinquency, promiscuity and alcoholism, and was, predictably, the product of a severely fractured home background. She became, in escaping thence, a footloose and fancy-free wandering sociopath, fair set to be attracted to the warmth of, and burned up by, the Klieg lights. There is some evidence that she was held captive by her torturer for the last week of her life. Despite floods of 'confessions' over the years, the identity of her captor and slayer – male or, it has been suggested, female, with involvement in a bisexual triangle – has remained impenetrable.

Prime source: *Contemporary newspapers.*

Identity unknown

The Bogle-Chandler Murders

Dr Gilbert Bogle

Margaret Chandler

Murderer: Unknown.

Victim: Dr. Gilbert Stanley Bogle (38). Margaret Olive Chandler (29): wife of Geoffrey Chandler,

Locus: Lane Cove River Park, Sydney, New South Wales.

Date: January 1st, 1963.

Means: Unknown. Presumption: Most likely some rare unidentifiable poison. A later suggestion: 'Japanese chocolate', yohimbine.

Motive: Unknown. Possibly jealousy. Revenge?

Crimewatch: Dr. Bogle was one of the world's top-flight physicists. He was also an unfaithful husband and a faithless philanderer. Any search for a motive must probe the widish arena of his sexual athleticism. At the time of his untimely demise, Gib Bogle's latest playmate was his friend Geoff Chandler's wife, Margaret. Boyle's wife, Vivienne, found bothering profitless. Geoff, who had a thing of his own going was not too bothered. After a New Year's Eve party, Gib and Margaret drove out to a secluded lovers' lane, in Cove River Park. All unknowing, they had a rendezvous with death. When found, Bogle's face was deep purple; a little blood trickled from his nose and the corner of his mouth. Margaret lay, mockingly half-clad, under the flattened cardboard sheets of a mouldy beer carton. The corpses were scrutinised down to the tiniest split-atom by batteries of doctors. They could find absolutely no reason why they should be dead. Neither was there any clue to the killer. But Mrs. Margaret Fowler, Gib's late passionate friend, herself a physicist married to a chemical engineer, cannot perhaps be so lightly dismissed as Dr. Gib dismissed her.

Prime sources: *The Bogle Mystery*, Stafford Silk, Howitz Publications, Sydney, 1963.
So You Think I Did It, Geoffrey Chandler, Sun Books, Melbourne, 1969.

Lizzie Andrew Borden

The Borden Murders

Accused: Lizzie Andrew Borden.
Victims: Abby Durfee Gray Borden (63): stepmother.
Andrew Jackson Borden (70): father.
Locus: 92 (now No. 230) Second Street, Fall River,
Massachusetts.
Date: August 4th, 1892.
Means: Bludgeoning with a hatchet.
Motive: Believed to have been to protect her and her
sister's inheritance – which she saw her father giving
away. Some would postulate hatred of her stepmother
and that Father had to be killed because he would
have known Lizzie to have been the murderer.
Crimewatch: It seems inconceivable that Lizzie
Borden should have walked out of the New Bedford
Courthouse with a not guilty verdict. And yet . . . the
perverseness of that New England jury has been
perpetuated by posterity. At least two other serious
candidates for the bloodstained laurels have been
proposed, Lizzie's elder sister, Emma (42), and
Bridget Sullivan (26), the Irish housemaid. And still
the freshly-bloodied pretenders keep popping up,
Old Uncle John Vinnicum and all. A terrible blow to
the unsullied virtue of Miss Lizzie was struck on the
September day, long after the trial, when she was
alleged to have shoplifted two porcelain paintings
from the stylish Tilden-Thurber store at Providence,
Rhode Island. Neither did her relationship with
actress Nance O'Neil, and its rumoured undertones
of lesbianism, improve the spinster Borden image in
the tight-lace Fall River community. Eyebrows were
raised, too, when, in 1904, Emma, who all her life had
watched over Lizzie like a little mother, and must

have known her guilt, left the home they shared. The sisters were never to see each other again. Lizzie died, not having properly recovered from a gall-bladder operation, aged 68, on June 1st, 1927, at Maplecroft, 7 French Street, Fall River. It was 34 years after her acquittal.

Prime sources: *The Fall River Tragedy,* Edwin H. Porter. Press of J. D. Munroe, Fall River, 1893. (Very scarce as Lizzie went round buying up and destroying all the copies she could lay her hands on.)
Trial of Lizzie Borden, Edmund Pearson, Doubleday, Doran, New York, 1937.
A Private Disgrace, Victoria Lincoln, G. P. Putnam's Sons, New York, 1967.
Goodbye Lizzie Borden, Robert Sullivan, Chatto & Windus, London, 1975.
Lizzie Borden: A Casebook of Family and Crime in the 1890s, edited by Joyce G. Williams, J. Eric Smithburn, M. Jeanne Peterson, T.I.S. Publications, Bloomington, Indiana, 1980.
Lizzie Borden: The Legend, The Truth, The Final Chapter, Arnold R. Brown, Rutledge Hill Press, Nashville, Tennessee, 1991.
Forty Whacks: New Evidence in the Life and Legend of Lizzie Borden, David Kent, Yankee Books/St. Martin's Press, U.S.A., 1992.

William Sidney Bradfield

The Main Line Murders

Dr. Jay Charles Smith

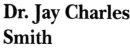

Murderers: William Sidney Bradfield. Dr. Jay Charles Smith.

Victims: Susan Reinert (*c.* 36). Karen Reinert (11): her daughter. Michael Reinert (10): her son. Also missing, since 1978, presumed dead (no criminal proceedings) are Jay Smith's troublesome daughter, Stephanie Smith Hunsberger, and her husband, Edward Hunsberger.

Locus: Not known. Susan Reinert's nude body, bruised and with chain marks, was found on June 25th, 1979, in the boot of her Plymouth Horizon in the car park of the Host Inn, Harrisburg, Pennsylvania. Karen and Michael were never found.

Date: On June 22nd, 1979, in a hailstorm, the three victims hurried out of their house at 662 Woodcrest Avenue, Ardmore, Pennsylvania, and were never seen alive again.

Means: Susan Reinert died from a dose of morphine.

Motive: Once smoke screen put up by Bradfield dispelled, more simple than it appeared. The 'Satanic rites' scenario, as mooted, was never a true runner, even if there was plenty of swinging sex going on in

the upper reaches of Upper Merion High School.
Despite his claims that he never sought to benefit,
Bradfield stood to gain under Susan Reinert's will and
life insurance policies of $730,000, and he *did* try to
get those monies in. Her children had to be killed
because they were eye-witnesses. Alternatively, they
were part of the murder plan *ab initio* in case through
the courts, *they* stood to gain. Motive not so clear for
Jay Smith. A share of the proceeds? Sadistic
enjoyment? Repayment of Bradfield's alibi for him at
his trial for robbery of a Sears, Roebuck store?

Crimewatch: Although convictions were obtained,
this case has never been fully fathomed. No
confessions. No knowing how to apportion the guilt
between the accomplices, or exactly when and where
the killings took place. Nicknamed 'The Prince of
Darkness', saturnine Dr. Smith, Colonel in the US
Army Reserve, behaved very strangely during his
tenure as principal at Upper Merion, but his mental
status was never at issue. Teacher Bill Bradfield,
obsessed with Ezra Pound, denied romantic
involvement with Susan Reinert and offered a shaky
alibi. In 1983, aged 50, he was convicted on three
counts of conspiracy to commit first-degree murder,
and sentenced to life imprisonment. Smith, aged 58,
was convicted in 1986 on three counts of first-degree
murder and sentenced to die by the electric chair.

Prime sources: *Engaged to Murder*, Loretta Schwartz-Nobel,
Viking, New York, 1987.
Echoes in the Darkness, Joseph Wambaugh, William Morrow,
New York, 1987.

Ian Brady

The Moors Murders

Serial killers

Myra Hindley

Murderers: Ian Brady. Myra Hindley.
Victims: John Kilbride (12) – Hindley convicted here only as accessory after the fact. Lesley Ann Downey (10). Edward Evans (17). Also: Pauline Reade (16) – No conviction. Keith Bennett (12) – No conviction.
Loci: Saddleworth Moor, Yorkshire (Kilbride, Reade, Bennett). 16 Wardle Brook Avenue, Hattersley, Manchester (Downey, Evans).
Dates: November 23rd, 1963 (Kilbride). December 26th, 1964 (Downey). October 6th 7th, 1965 (Evans). July 12th, 1963 (Reade). June 16th, 1964 (Bennett).
Means: According to Hindley's confession, Brady told her that he strangled the boy with a thin piece of string (Kilbride). According to Hindley's confession, Brady strangled the girl with a piece of string (Downey). Hacking with a hatchet and strangulation with an electric flex (Evans). The throat was cut (Reade). According to Hindley's confession, Brady told her that he strangled the boy with a piece of string (Bennett).
Motive: Pleasure in killing. Power. Sadism. Sexual gratification, with actual sexual interference by Brady.
Crimewatch: According to Hindley's confession to

Detective Chief Superintendent Peter Topping in 1987, her rôle, as Brady's creature, was not to participate in the killings, but to abduct the victims. Thus, John Kilbride went 'like a little lamb to the slaughter.' In the cases of Reade and Bennett, the DPP decided against a new trial, although both Brady and Hindley had implicated themselves by their statements to Topping, and by helping the police, more than twenty years later, to search for the two graves on Saddleworth Moor. Pauline Reade's body found July 1st, 1987. Keith Bennett still lies hidden. Brady has also confessed to five other murders, but the police have not been able to substantiate his claims: he 'bricked' a man on wasteland behind Piccadilly Railway Station, Manchester; he stabbed a man under the railway arches in the Calton area of Glasgow; he threw a woman into the canal near the Rembrandt public-house, Manchester; he shot and buried an 18-year-old youth on Saddleworth Moor; he shot a hiker at Loch Long, Scotland, and buried him. Brady, born January 2nd, 1938, is said to be suffering from a paranoid psychosis. He is held at Park Lane Hospital, Liverpool. Hindley, born July 23rd, 1942, is at Cookham Wood Prison, Rochester, Kent.

Prime sources: *The Moor Murders,* David Marchbanks, Leslie Frewin, London, 1966.
The Monsters of the Moors, John Deane Potter, Elek, London, 1966.
Satan's Children, Judge Gerald Sparrow, Odhams, London, 1966.
Beyond Belief, Emlyn Williams, Hamish Hamilton, London, 1967.
On Iniquity, Pamela Hansford Johnson, Macmillan, London, 1967.
The Trial of Ian Brady and Myra Hindley, edited by Jonathan Goodman, David & Charles, Newton Abbot, 1973.
Devil's Disciples, Robert Wilson, Express Newspapers, London, 1986.
Brady and Hindley, Fred Harrison, Ashgrove Press, Bath, 1986.
Return to Hell, Robert Wilson, Javelin Books, London, 1988.
Myra Hindley, Jean Ritchie, Angus & Robertson, London, 1988.
For the Love of Lesley, Ann West. W. H. Allen, London, 1989.
Topping, Peter Topping, Angus & Robertson, London, 1989.

Identity unknown

The Bravo Mystery

Florence Bravo

Murderer: Unknown.
Victim: Charles Delauney Turner Bravo (30).
Locus: The Priory, Bedford Hill Road (now Bedford Hill), Balham, London.
Date: April 21st, 1876.
Means: Antimony (Tartar emetic).
Motive: Elimination.
Crimewatch: Charles Bravo, Barrister-at-Law, penny-pinching second husband of less than five months of wealthy Florence Ricardo (30), went upstairs to bed in their beautiful Strawberry Hill gothic home, The Priory, somewhere about a quarter past nine on the night of April 18th, 1876, rushed forth from his bedroom in his nightshirt shouting for hot water to drink, and three days after that was dead of antimony. Accident? Suicide? Murder? If the latter (and it almost certainly was), there were three popular suspects – the widow, the widow's companion-housekeeper, Mrs. Jane Cannon Cox (49), and the widow's erstwhile 'ancient lover', 68-year-old Dr. James Manby Gully, wizard of the Malvern water cure. There was a 'trial by inquest', from which Mrs. Bravo and Mrs. Cox emerged as equal favourites so far as the public was concerned, but neither attracting the further interest or action of the law. Type specimen of a nineteenth-century *cause scandaleuse,* the Bravo affair has matured into one of the great, abiding Victorian murder mysteries. A tragic figure, Florence did not long survive Bravo, dying, like her first husband Lieutenant Alexander Ricardo, of drink, at Coombe Lodge, Southsea, Hampshire, on September 17th, 1878.

Prime sources: *The Balham Mystery: or, The 'Bravo' Poisoning Case,* Broadsheet issued in seven weekly parts, 1876.
The Bravo Case, F. J. P. Veale, The Merrymeade Publishing Co. Ltd, Brighton, 1950.
How Charles Bravo Died, Yseult Bridges, Jarrolds, London, 1956.
Suddenly at the Priory, John Williams, Heinemann, London, 1957.
Murder at the Priory, Bernard Taylor and Kate Clarke, Grafton Books, London, 1988.

Jerome Henry Brudos

Serial killer

Murderer: Jerome Henry Brudos.
Victims: Linda K. Slawson (19). Jan Susan Whitney (23). Karen Elena Sprinker (19). Linda Dawn Salee (22).
Locus: 3123 Center Street, Salem, Oregon. Brudos' home. In the basement there (Slawson). In the garage workshop (Whitney, Sprinker, Salee).
Dates: January 26th, 1968 (Slawson). November 26th, 1968 (Whitney). March 27th, 1968 (Sprinker) April 23rd, 1969 (Salee).
Means: Strangulation.
Motive: To be the man who had power over women. Expressing hatred of women and reaping sexual gratification.
Crimewatch: Brudos hated, and was disliked by, his mother, who repeatedly compared him disadvantageously with his brother. He early exhibited aberrant traits. First shoe fetishism. Graduated to female underwear fetishism, stealing from clothes-lines and enjoying dressing up in them. In 1956, aged 17, committed to Oregon State Mental Hospital, Salem, for beating up a girl. Joined US Army, March 1959. Discharged on psychiatric grounds, October. A skilled electrician, married Darcie Metzler (17). Two children. Overbearing, though not unkind, husband, but his sexual psychopathy accelerating. Prior to 1968, had beaten, choked and raped, but never killed. Then murdered four women. Thought to have killed a fifth – Stephanie Vilcko (16) – but no firm proof. By now, full-blown, dangerous sexual psychopath, exhibiting sadism and necrophilia. Photographed victims before and after death. Cut breasts from

Whitney and Sprinker to make paper-weights, and the left foot from Slawson, which he kept in the freezer, to try high-heeled shoes on it. Kept also Whitney's body hanging from the ceiling of his workshop and used to have intercourse with it after work. Sentenced to life in Oregon State Prison, 1969.

Prime source: *Lust Killer*, Andy Stack (Ann Rule), New American Library, New York, 1983.

Theodore (Ted) Robert Bundy

The Campus Killer
Serial killer

Murderer: Theodore (Ted) Robert Bundy.
Victims: At least 23, possibly 40, girls; perhaps even more.
Loci: Washington, Oregon, Utah, Colorado, Florida.
Dates: April 1st, 1974 – September 2nd, 1978.
Means: Usually bludgeoning, also strangling.
Motive: Sexual gratification: there was multiple perversion.
Crimewatch: Unable to cope with his illegitimacy, voyeur, psychology graduate, law student, not such a genius as he imagined (IQ 124), Bundy was a personable, plausible chameleon, at home on campuses and expert at vanishing girls away. Happiest in a Volkswagen, he kept on the move, and twice he escaped from custody. His personality began to disintegrate. He entered the Chi Omega sorority house, Florida State University, Tallahassee, and moved from room to room laying about him with a cudgel. His final known victim, Kimberley Leach, was only twelve years old. In court in Miami in 1979, he enjoyed the glamour of defending himself. Bite marks on a body were powerfully evidential, and he was sent to Death Row. On January 24th, 1989, he was electrocuted, aged 42, at Florida State Prison.

Prime sources: *The Stranger Beside Me,* Ann Rule, W. W. Norton, New York, 1980.
Bundy: The Deliberate Stranger, Richard W. Larsen, Prentice Hall, New Jersey, 1980.
The Phantom Prince: My Life With Ted Bundy, Elizabeth Kendall, Madrona, Seattle, 1981.
The Only Living Witness, Stephen G. Michaud and Hugh Aynesworth, Simon & Schuster, New York, 1983.
Ted Bundy: Conversations With a Killer, Stephen G. Michaud and Hugh Aynesworth, Signet Books, New York, 1989.

William Burke

The Edinburgh Body Snatchers

Mass murderers

William Hare

Murderers: William Burke. William Hare.
Victims: Certainly 16. Very likely 17. Possibly more.
Loci;   Known loci – Log's Lodgings, Tanner's Close, West Port, Edinburgh, and Gibbs Close, Canongate, Edinburgh.
Date: 1828.
Means: Smothering or 'burking'.
Motive: Simple, straightforward financial gain.
Crimewatch: Wrongly styled body-snatchers. They murderously manufactured the goods they purveyed to the medical schools. Both men were Irish, though they practised in Scotland. Burke hanged January 28th, 1829. He was 36. Pieces of the rope sold at 2s. 6d. per inch. Burke's skeleton and a pocket-book bound in his flayed skin are preserved in Edinburgh medical collections. Forget the old canard about Hare, who was around the same age as Burke at the time of the murders, ending up as a blind beggar on the north side of London's Oxford Street.

Prime sources: *Trial of William Burke and Helen M'Dougal (With Supplement),* John MacNee, Robert Buchanan, Edinburgh, 1829.

The Westport Murders, Anon, Thomas Ireland, Edinburgh, 1829.

The History of Burke and Hare, George MacGregor, Thomas D. Morison, Glasgow, 1884.

Notable British Trial, edited by William Roughead, William Hodge, Edinburgh, 1921.

Burke and Hare: The True Story, Hugh Douglas, Robert Hale, London, 1973.

Burke and Hare: The Resurrection Men, Jacques Barzun, The Scarecrow Press, Metuchen, New Jersey, 1974.

Burke and Hare, Owen Dudley Edwards, Polygon Books, Edinburgh, 1980.

Frederick Edward Francis Bywaters

Edith Jessie Thompson

Murderers: Frederick Edward **Francis** Bywaters. Edith Jessie Thompson.

Victim: Percy Thompson (32); husband of Edith.

Locus: Belgrave Road, Ilford, Essex: along which the Thompsons were walking home to 41 Kensington Gardens shortly after midnight, returning from a visit to the theatre.

Date: October 4th, 1922.

Means: Stabbing – by the hand of Bywaters.

Motive: Elimination of husband for amatory ends.

Crimewatch: The jury believed that Edith Thompson had incited her lover to murder her husband. Her love-letters, which Bywaters, a ship's writer, had preserved in a locked box on the SS *Morea,* made sinister reference to powdered glass and poison, although the post-mortem, conducted by Sir Bernard Spilsbury, proved negative on those matters. Both Edith Thompson (28) and Frederick Bywaters (20) were hanged at 9 a.m. on January 9th, 1923, she at Holloway Prison, he at Pentonville. It has been suggested that she might have been pregnant.

Prime sources: *Notable British Trial,* edited by Filson Young, William Hodge, Edinburgh, 1923.
The Innocence of Edith Thompson, Lewis Broad, Hutchinson, London, 1952.
Bywaters and Mrs. Thompson, Ernest Dudley, Odhams Press, London, 1953.
Criminal Justice, René Weis, Hamish Hamilton, London, 1988.

James Camb

Murderer: James Camb.
Victim: Eileen Isabella Ronnie 'Gay' Gibson (21).
Locus: Cabin 126, Union Castle liner *Durban Castle*.
Date: October 18th, 1947.
Means: Probably strangulation.
Motive: Can be only conjectural: e.g. concealment of rape, or plain sadistic murder, in a man who had previously attacked three women on shipboard.
Crimewatch: Camb (31) admitted disposing of the body of the attractive young actress, to whose cabin he had paid a secret visit that night, by pushing it out through the porthole. His defence was that she had died of natural causes – a fit – during voluntary sexual intercourse with him, and that he had panicked. Scratches were found on his wrists. He was convicted of murder, sentenced to death, reprieved and sentenced to life imprisonment in 1948. Released on licence in 1959, he was in trouble in May 1967 for indecent assault on an eight-year-old girl. He was put on probation for two years. But in May 1971, found guilty of 'lewd, indecent and libidinous practices' towards three young girls, he was sent back to prison. Finally released in 1978, suffering with heart trouble. Died July 7th, 1979. He was then known as James Clarke.

Prime sources: *Notable British Trial*, edited by Geoffrey Clark, William Hodge, Edinburgh, 1949.
The Girl in the Stateroom, Charles Boswell and Lewis Thompson, Gold Medal Books, New York, 1951.
The Porthole Murder Case, Denis Herbstein, Hodder & Stoughton, London, 1991.

Patrick Carraher

Murderer: Patrick Carraher.
Victims: James Sydney Emden Shaw (23). John Gordon, junior (39).
Loci: Junction of Ballater and Thistle Streets in the Gorbals district of Glasgow (Shaw). In Taylor Street, near McAslin Street, in the Townhead district of Glasgow (Gordon).
Dates: August 14th, 1938 (Shaw). November 23rd, 1945 (Gordon).
Means: Stabbing.
Motive: Relief of drunken aggression.
Crimewatch: Twice tried for murder in Glasgow. Petty criminal denizen of the Gorbals. Product of the sub-world of McArthur and Long's *No Mean City*. A street brawler. Violent. More violent in drink. Fatal stabbing of the young soldier, Shaw, reduced to charge of culpable homicide *(Anglice:* manslaughter). Sentenced to three years' penal servitude. Defence based on psychopathy, alcoholism, 'persecution mania' and diminished responsibility (then available only in Scotland) failed and, for the murder of Gordon, he was hanged at Barlinnie Prison, Glasgow, on April 6th, 1946. Carraher was 39 years old.

Prime source: *Notable British Trial,* edited by George Blake, William Hodge, Edinburgh, 1951.

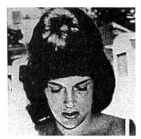

Alice Lynne (Lindy) Chamberlain

The Dingo Baby Case

Accused: Alice Lynne (Lindy) Chamberlain. Pastor Michael Chamberlain: husband.

Victim: Azaria Chantel Loren: daughter, aged nine weeks.

Locus: Ayers Rock, Northern Territory, Central Australia.

Date: August 17th, 1980.

Means: Suggested: cutting of neck with sharp instrument, such as small pair of scissors. Necessarily conjectural, based on bloodstain pattern on discovered garment, as body never bound.

Motive: Unknown. Prosecution unable to offer any. Mrs. Chamberlain's doctor negated explanation of post-natal depression.

Crimewatch: Baby allegedly carried off from tent by wild dingo. Scientific evidence held to contradict this scenario. Bafflingly controversial case. February 2nd, 1986, Azaria's matinée jacket found. June 2nd, 1987, the Chamberlains' convictions quashed and they were acquitted. But argument still divides Australia.

Prime sources: *Azaria: Wednesday's Child,* James Simmonds, TPNL Books, Melbourne, 1982.

The Dingo Baby Case, Richard Shears, Sphere Books, London, 1982.

Evil Angels, John Bryson, Viking, Penguin Books, Australia, 1985.

The Dingo Baby Case, Ken Crispin, Lion Publishing, Tring, England, 1987.

Innocence Regained, Norman H. Young, The Federation press, Annandale, New South Wales, 1989.

Through my Eyes, Lindy Chamberlain, William Heinemann, Australia, 1990, London, 1991.

Eugène Marie Chantrelle

Murderer: Eugène Marie Chantrelle.
Victim: Elizabeth Cullen Dyer or Chantrelle (25): wife.
Locus: 81a George Street, Edinburgh.
Date: January 2nd, 1878.
Means: Poison. Probably opium. Administered on a piece of orange and/or in lemonade.
Motive: Elimination, plus gain. Wife insured for £1,000
Crimewatch: Extremely nasty, luxuriantly hirsute venefic. A Frenchman. Born at Nantes in 1834. A gifted linguist, followed the profession of teacher in England, where he was jailed for nine months for 'an outrage of a very gross nature' upon one of his pupils. He repeated this free French sexual liberalism while, in 1867, teaching at Newington Academy, a private school in Edinburgh. Having seduced and impregnated her, he was constrained to marry his unfortunate 15-year-old pupil, Elizabeth Cullen Dyer. She bore him four sons. Brutal and dipsomaniacal, he treated the poor young woman shamefully for ten years – first at No. 95 and then No. 81a George Street, and on holiday at 17 Pitt Street, Portobello. He tried to blame her death on a leaking gas-pipe in the bedroom. His was the first non-public execution to take place in Scotland, being carried out *within* the Calton Jail, Edinburgh, on May 31st, 1878. He made no confession. Wife buried, grave T118, Grange Cemetery, Edinburgh.

Prime source: *Notable Scottish Trial*, edited by A. Duncan Smith, William Hodge, Edinburgh, 1906.

George Chapman, properly Severin Klosowski
The Borough Poisoner
Mass murderer

Murderer: George Chapman, properly Severin Klosowski.

Victims: Mary Isabella Spink (41): masquerading as 'wife'. Elizabeth Taylor (36): masquerading as 'wife'. Maud Eliza Marsh (19): masquerading as 'wife'.

Loci: Prince of Wales Tavern, Bartholomew Square, Finsbury, London (Spink). Monument Tavern, Union Street, Borough, South-East London (Taylor). Crown public-house, Union Street, Borough, South-East London (Marsh).

Dates: December 25th, 1897 (Spink). February 13th, 1901 (Taylor). October 22nd, 1902 (Taylor).

Means. Antimony in all three cases

Motive: Desire for a change of quasi-matrimonial partner, with a clawing-in of any financial pickings on the way. An element of sadism may have been attached.

Crimewatch: Parallel facts of timing and abode can be adduced to argue that Chapman was really Jack the Ripper under another hat, operating domestically after the East End streets had become too hot for his pleasures. Inspector Abberline it was who first raised this no longer fashionable hare, congratulating Chapman's arresting officer, Inspector Godley, 'You've got Jack the Ripper at last.' Chapman's exotic background was persuasive. In origin he was a Russian Pole, a feldscher or barber-surgeon. Not a frank madman, but reckless, lively, libidinous, cunning cyclist with the police cycling club, photographer of his besotted victims. Born on December 14th, 1865. Hanged at Wandsworth on April 7th, 1903.

Prime source: *Notable British Trial*, edited by H. L. Adam, William Hodge, Edinburgh, 1930.

John Reginald Halliday Christie

Serial killer

Murderer: John Reginald Halliday Christie.
Victims: Ruth Margarete Christine Fuerst (21). Muriel Amelia Eady (32). Beryl Susanna Evans (20): fellow-tenant. (?). Geraldine Evans: Beryl's 13-month-old baby. (?). Ethel Christie (54): wife. Kathleen Maloney (26). Rita Nelson (24). Hectorina MacLennan (26).
Locus: 10 Rillington Place (later re-named Ruston Close), Notting Hill, London.
Dates: August 1943 (Fuerst). October 1944 (Eady). November 8th, 1949 (Evans). November 10th, 1949 (Geraldine Evans). December 14th, 1952 (Ethel Christie). January 1953 (Maloney). January 1953 (Nelson). March 6th, 1953 (MacLennan).
Means: Strangulation with a ligature.
Motive: Generally, sexual gratification with necrophilia. In the case of Mrs. Christie, plain elimination. Baby Geraldine was killed because her motherless presence would have been incriminating.
Crimewatch: Timothy John Evans was hanged at Pentonville on March 9th, 1950, for the murder of his daughter, Geraldine. He had confessed to killing both his wife and daughter, whose bodies were found in the washhouse, although he later retracted and blamed Christie. On March 24th, 1953, the bodies of Maloney, Nelson and MacLennan were discovered in a papered-over alcove in the kitchen. Mrs. Christie's body was under the floorboards of the ground-floor front room. The skeletons of Fuerst and Eady were dug up from the garden. Christie confessed to the murder of Beryl Evans, but not to that of Geraldine. The apportionment of guilt is still hotly debated.

Christie (born April 8th, 1898) was hanged at
Pentonville on July 15th, 1953. On October 18th,
1966 Evans was granted a posthumous free pardon.

Prime sources: *Medical and Scientific Investigations in the
Christie Case,* Medical Publications Limited, London, 1953.
*Home Office Report: The Deaths of Mrs. Beryl Evans and Geraldine
Evans,* by. J. Scott Henderson, Q.C., Her Majesty's Stationery
Office, July 1953, Cmd. 8896
Supplementary Report: The Case of Timothy John Evans, by Mr. J.
Scott Henderson, Q.C., Her Majesty's Stationery Office,
September 1953, Cmd. 8946.
*The Man on Your Conscience? An Investigation of the Evans
Murder Trial,* Michael Eddowes, Cassell, London, 1955.
Notable British Trial, edited by F. Tennyson Jesse, William
Hodge, Edinburgh, 1957.
The Christie Case, Ronald Maxwell, R. S. Gray, London, nd.
The Two Stranglers of Rillington Place, Rupert Furneaux,
Panther Books, London, 1961.
Ten Rillington Place, Ludovic Kennedy, Gollancz, London,
1961.
The Case of Timothy John Evans, Home Office Report of an
Inquiry by The Hon. Mr. Justice Brabin, Her Majesty's
Stationery Office, October 1966, Cmnd. 3101.

Douglas Daniel Clark

The Sunset Slayer
Serial killer

Murderer: Douglas Daniel Clark.
Victims: Marnette Comer (17). Gina Marano (15).
Cynthia Chandler (16): Marano's step-sister, Exxie
Wilson (20). Karen Jones (24). Sixth unidentified
young girl.
Loci: A ravine near Sylmar, San Fernando Valley:
mummified body found June 30th, 1980 (Comer).
Along a Los Angeles highway exit road, two bodies
found June 12th, 1980 (Marano, Chandler). Studio
City – Burbank area of LA. In sedate Burbank
neighbourhood, body found June 24th, 1980 (Jones).
In an alley, headless body found, June 24th, 1980
(Wilson). Missing head found June 27th, in wooden
box in the driveway of a Burbank resident's home.
Saugus-Newhall area of LA. Body of a nude girl
discovered March 2nd, 1981.
Dates: June 1st, 1980 (Comer). June 11th, 1980
(Marano, Chandler). June 24th, 1980 (Wilson, Jones).
Date unknown (unidentified girl).
Means: Shooting with small-calibre gun.
Motive: Enjoyment of perverse sexual practices, with
attendant necrophilia.
Crimewatch: Clark, a 34-year-old boilermaker, and
his mistress, Carol Mary Bundy (37), a nurse, spent
the summer of 1980 cruising Hollywood's Sunset
Boulevard in his station wagon looking for young
women – prostitutes, 'mysteries', runaways – to sate
Clark's kinky appetite. His particular fancy was to
shoot a girl through the head at the climax of fellatio.
He would then strip her of her underwear, to be
saved as a potent trophy, have intercourse with the
corpse and, the ultimate refinement, carry away her

severed head to be subsequently made-up like a
Barbie doll by Bundy and used as an object of sexual
gratification. On August 9th, 1980, the headless body
of John Robert Murray (45), Bundy's former
boyfriend, was found in his parked car a few streets
from his Van Nuys home. He had been shot and
stabbed many times. Bundy was arrested. Pursuing a
tip-off, police arrested Clark – August 11th – charged
him on six counts of murder and with aiding and
abetting Bundy. He tried to blame all the killings on
her and Jack Murray, declaring the couple were Ted
Bundy copy-cat killers. Changing her plea of not
guilty by reason of insanity to guilty, Bundy, mother of
two, drew a 52 years to life sentence. Clark,
condemned to the San Quentin gas chamber on
March·16th, 1983, told the jury, 'I don't march to the
same drummer as you do.'

Prime source: *The Sunset Murders,* Louise Farr, Pocket Books,
Simon & Schuster, New York, 1992.

Identity unknown

The Cleveland Butcher Serial killer

Frank Dolezal – Was he the Cleveland Butcher?

Murderer: Identity unknown.
Victims: Official body count: 12 victims. Speculatively: 13-40. The official 12 are Edward Andrassy, Florence Sawdey Polillo, Rose Wallace and 6 unknown men and 3 unknown women.
Loci: In and around Cleveland, Ohio. Kingsbury Run, Jackass Hill, at East 4th Street (Andrassy and Body 2, unknown male). 2315 East 20th Street, alley behind (Polillo). Kingsbury Run, Woodland Avenue and East 51st Street (Body 4, tattooed male). Big Creek, near Clinton Road, Brooklyn (Body 5, male). Kingsbury Run, stagnant pool below East 37th Street bridge (Body 6, male). Shore of Lake Erie, beach at foot of East 156th Street (Body 7, female). Under east portion of Lorain-Carnegie Bridge (Wallace). In Cuyahoga River at West 3rd Street and Erie Railroad (Body 9, male). In Cuyahoga River near Superior Avenue (Body 10, female). Intersection of East 9th Street and Shore Drive (Body 11, female, and Body 12, male).
Dates: September 23rd, 1935 (Andrassy and Body 2). January 26th, 1936 (Florence Polillo). June 5th, 1936 (Body 4, male). July 22nd, 1936 (Body 5, male). September 10th, 1936 (Body 6, male). February 23rd, 1937 (Body 7, female). June 5th, 1937 (Wallace). July 6th, 1937 (Body 9, male). April 8th, 1938 (Body 10, female).August 16th, 1938 (Body 11, female and Body 12, male).
Means: Decapitation. Retracted neck muscles indicate at or immediately after death.
Motive: Probably sheer *lustmord*. Sadistic pleasure with bizarrely variable sexual psychopathy. Three of

the males emasculated.

Crimewatch: Brilliant knife-work suggested skill in the wielding of lethal cutlery. Inexplicably, supply of headless torsos suddenly dried up in Cleveland in 1938. But six more turned up in neighbouring Pennsylvania 1938-42. Prime suspect, Frank Dolezal, 52-year-old Bohemian bricklayer. Hanged himself in jail in August 1939. Eliot Ness believed killer to be 'Gaylord Sundheim' – pseudonym for young man of influential family.

Prime sources: *Cleveland Murders*, edited by Oliver Weld Bayer, Duell, Sloan & Pearce, New York, 1947.
Butcher's Dozen, John B. Martin, Harper & Brothers, New York, 1950.
Torso, Steven Nickel, John F. Blair, Winston-Salem, North Carolina, 1989.

Dr. Carl A. Coppolino

Murderer: Dr. Carl A. Coppolino.
Victim: Dr. Carmela Coppolino (32): wife.
Locus: 591 Bowsprit Lane, Longboat Key, Sarasota, Florida.
Date: August 28th, 1965.
Means: Injection of succinylcholine chloride (a muscle relaxant used in anaesthesiology).
Motive: The theory was that Coppolino wished to be free to remarry. There was also a life insurance of $65,000.
Crimewatch: Coppolino (born May 13th, 1932) was twice tried for murder upon the information of a discarded, older mistress, Marjorie Farber. A jury in Freehold, New Jersey, in December 1966, did not believe her evidence that Dr. Coppolino had hypnotised her into a continuous waking trance, during which, on July 30th, 1963, he tried to influence her to inject her sleeping husband, Lieutenant-Colonel William E. Farber, with succinylcholine chloride. She further stated that Coppolino himself finished him off with a pillow. Dr. Carmela Coppolino signed the death certificate, entering coronary thrombosis. For the State, Dr. Milton Helpern found at autopsy no evidence of such thrombosis, and a normal heart for a man of fifty-two. However, he *did* find that the cricoid cartilage in the larynx was fractured. F. Lee Bailey, for the defence, argued that the injury occurred post mortem, during the process of late exhumation. Freed, Dr. Coppolino was again put up in Naples, Florida, in April 1967. This time he was charged with murdering his own wife, on August 28th, 1965, by use of the same drug.

The death certificate specified coronary occlusion.
Three weeks later, widowed Dr. Coppolino married
Mary Gibson, and the following day, Marjorie Farber
went to the authorities. Carmela's body, too, was
exhumed, and Dr. Helpern found no evidence of any
disease whatsoever. There was an apparent needle
puncture in the left buttock. The toxicological
evidence regarding succinylcholine chloride in the
exhumed body was unsatisfactory, but the jury
accepted it. Coppolino was convicted of second-
degree murder and sentenced to life imprisonment.
On October 16th, 1979, he was released on lifetime
parole, for exemplary behaviour, and, in 1980,
produced his own remarkable book about the events
(and the atrocious prison conditions in Florida) in
which he made worrying inroads into the medical
evidence for the State.

Prime sources: *The Trials of Dr. Coppolino,* Paul Holmes, The
New American Library, New York, 1968.
No Deadly Drug, John D. MacDonald, Doubleday, New York,
1968.
The Crime That Never Was, Carl A. Coppolino, M.D. Justice
Press, Inc., Florida, 1980

Dean Arnold Corll

Serial killer

Murderer: Dean Arnold Corll.
Victims: At least 27 teenage boys.
Loci: A succession of Houston addresses, according to Corll's two accomplices (see below). 3300 Yorktown. 6363 San Felipe. 3200 Mangum. 915 Columbia Street. 925 Schuler Street. 904 Westcott Towers. 1855 Wirt Road. And in Pasadena, at 2020 Lamar Drive.
Dates: 1970-73.
Means: Strangling and shooting.
Motive: Sexual gratification, with torture and mutilation.
Crimewatch: Corll, born in 1939, electrician and hander-out of candy, seduced two much younger accomplices, Elmer Wayne Henley and David Owen Brooks, and used them to procure boys from the Heights section of Houston. A pine 'torture-board' with handcuffs was the basis of Corll's equipment. The lost boys were buried under a boathouse, No. 11 Southwest Boat Storage, Silver Shell Road, Houston, at Lake Sam Rayburn, and at High Island Beach. In a final showdown on August 8th, 1973, Henley shot Corll dead, before Corll killed him. Henley (born 1956) and Brooks (born 1955) were convicted at San Antonio of six murders and were sentenced to life imprisonment.

Prime sources: *Mass Murder in Houston,* John K. Gurwell, Cordovan Press, Houston, 1974.
The Man With the Candy, Jack Olsen, Simon & Schuster, New York, 1974.

Juan Vallejo Corona

Serial killer

Murderer: Juan Vallejo Corona.
Victims: 25 men of all ages.
Locus: On and around the Sullivan Ranch, near Yuba City, California.
Dates: Over about six weeks up to May, 1971.
Means: Stabbing, hacking the heads with a machete, and shooting.
Motive: These were homosexual lust murders.
Crimewatch: Fifteen years earlier, Corona had received in-patient treatment for full-blown schizophrenia, from which he had appeared to make a good recovery. Married, with children, he was a respected labour contractor, domiciled at 768 Richland Road, County of Sutter, hiring crews of men to harvest the ripe Californian crops. He put itinerant workers up in a bunkhouse at the Sullivan Ranch, and in shallow graves dug, sometimes in advance, in the burgeoning orchards, he laid their desecrated bodies – vagrants, hoboes, winos, not likely to be missed. But he scattered clues like fallen fruit, and even kept a ledger containing the names of the slain. He was sentenced, aged 38, to twenty-five terms of life imprisonment. In prison he was stabbed 32 times and blinded in one eye. On successful appeal that he should have pleaded insanity, rather than denial which included alibi, he was moved to an institution for the criminally insane.

Prime sources: *Burden of Proof,* Ed Cray, Macmillan, New York, 1973.
The Road to Yuba City, Tracy Kidder, Doubleday, New York, 1974.
Jury: The People vs. *Juan Corona,* Victor Villaseñor, Little, Brown and Company, Boston, 1977.

Richard Francis Cottingham

The Times Square Torso Murders
Serial killer

Murderer: Richard Francis Cottingham.
Victims: Maryann Carr (26). Deedeh Goodarzi.
Unidentified female. Valorie Ann Street (19). Jean
Mary Ann Reyner (25).
Loci: Locus of killing not known. Scream heard at
victim's home – Apartment 112, Building 462,
Ledgewood Terrace Apartments, Liberty Street,
Little Ferry, New Jersey. Body found on parking lot of
the Quality Inn, Hasbrouck Heights, New Jersey
(Carr). Room 417, Travel Inn Motor Hotel, 515 West
42nd Street, Manhattan, New York (Goodarzi and
Unidentified). Room 132, Quality Inn, Hasbrouck
Heights, New Jersey (Street). Room 1139, Hotel
Seville, East 29th Street, New York (Reyner).
Dates: December 15th, 1977 (Carr). December 2nd,
1979 (Goodarzi and Unidentified). May 4th, 1980
(Street). May 15th, 1980 (Reyner).
Means: Strangulation with a ligature. The lungs had
collapsed: suffocated? Mouth was taped, and hands
and legs handcuffed (Carr). Both bodies found badly
burned, on twin beds, with their heads and hands
missing. The severed parts were never discovered
(Goodarzi and Unidentified). Strangled. Nude body
stuffed under bed. Handcuffed, beaten, bitten and
raped. Mouth sealed with adhesive tape (Street).
Strangled and stabbed. Then breasts cut off and body
set on fire (Reyner).
Motive: The facts speak for themselves.
Crimewatch: Cottingham, born November 25th,
1946, married, computer operator, was arrested in
mid-flow at his favourite torture-ground, the Quality
Inn, Hasbrouck Heights. There, on May 22nd, 1980,

in Room 117, for three hours he had been enjoying himself with 18-year-old Leslie Ann O'Dell, until her screams were heard. He ran away but was caught by a police officer. In his 'Trophy Room' at his home at 29 Vreeland Street, Lodi, New Jersey, clothing, jewellery, perfume, motel keys and purses were found. Maryann Carr was a nurse, but the rest of the murder victims were prostitutes. There were a number of other near-murders. Frightened girls testified that Cottingham had first drugged them with barbiturates. He was a savage biter, who went for the girls' breasts. Sentenced to life imprisonment after three separate trials.

Prime source: *The Prostitute Murders,* Rod Leith, Lyle Stuart, Secaucus, New Jersey, 1983.

Mary Ann Cotton

Mass murderer

Murderer: Mary Ann Cotton.
Victims: Mass murderer – of her nearest and dearest. Some children might have died of natural causes, but 21 persons perished. William Mowbray, her first husband. Her 8 (or 9) children of that union. George Ward, her second husband. Margaret Stott, her own mother. John, James and Elizabeth Robinson, her stepchildren by her third husband, James Robinson. Mary Isabella Robinson, her first child by James Robinson. Frederick Cotton, her bigamous fourth husband. Margaret Cotton, Frederick Cotton's sister. Frederick Cotton and Charles Edward Cotton, Cotton's two sons. Robert Robson Cotton, her own child by Cotton. Joseph Nattras, a lover.
Locus: County Durham, England.
Date: c. 1852-72
Means: *Arsenic.*
Motive: Financial gain from life insurance policies. Freedom to change marital partner.
Crimewatch: Legendary Victorian bogey-woman. Administered arsenic brew in strong tea, having acquired the poison allegedly to anoint bed-legs against bugs. Ten-year-old Frederick Cotton, on his death-bed asked to be coffined in his black glengarry cap. In Mary Cotton's defence, it was put that arsenic had been taken in from exudate of green wallpaper. Hanged – and it was botched – at Durham Prison on March 24th, 1873, aged 40.

Prime source: *Mary Ann Cotton,* Arthur Appleton, Michael Joseph, London, 1973.

Dr. Thomas Neill Cream

Serial killer

Murderer: Dr. Thomas Neill Cream.
Victims: Daniel Stott, (c. 61). Ellen Donworth (19).
Matilda Clover (27). Alice Marsh (21). Emma Shrivell
(18).
Loci: Grand Prairie, Boone County, Illinois (Stott).
Waterloo Road, South-East London (Donworth). 27
Lambeth Road, South-East London (Clover). 118
Stamford Street, South-East London (Marsh and
Shrivell).
Dates: June 14th, 1881 (Stott). October 13th, 1891
(Donworth). October 21st, 1891 (Clover). April 12th,
1892 (Marsh and Shrivell).
Means: Strychnine.
Motive: The sadistic pleasure of dosing unsuspecting
prostitutes with a painful poison. Cream did not witness
their sufferings, so the enjoyment must have come with
the passing of the poison to the victim, and in the
imagination thereafter.
Crimewatch: Donald Rumbelow in *The Complete Jack the
Ripper* annihilates the old legend that Dr. Cream was
really Jack the Ripper and confessed so to Mr. Hangman
Billington. At the material time Cream was incarcerated
in the Illinois State Penitentiary at Joliet, for the murder
by strychnine of Daniel Stott, husband of Cream's
mistress. Although Cream's relatives may have thought
him to be insane, and although he may have been in the
habit of taking morphia, he was not McNaghten-mad.
He knew the nature and quality of his acts, and he
certainly fooled his fiancée, Miss Laura Sabbatini, of
Chapel Street, Berkhamstead. On November 15th, 1892
(aged 42). Cream was hanged at Newgate.

Prime source: *Notable British Trial*, edited by W. Teignmouth
Shore, William Hodge, Edinburgh, 1923.

Dr. Hawley Harvey Crippen

Murderer: Dr. Hawley Harvey Crippen.
Victim: Cora Crippen née Kunigunde Mackamotzki, stage-name Belle Elmore (c.34): wife.
Locus: 39 Hilldrop Crescent, Camden, North London.
Date: February 1st, 1910.
Means: Hyoscine.
Motive: Elimination of a burdensome wife in favour of a new loved one: Ethel Clara le Neve.
Crimewatch: The degree of premeditation is still arguable, the method of administration of hyoscine open to discussion. It is debated that the poison was given merely to quench Cora Crippen's unappreciated libido. Crippen buried the dismembered corpse in quick-lime under the cellar floor, imported Ethel into the household, arrayed her in his wife's finery, and inserted a notice of his wife's death in California in the *Era*. Suspicion forced an urgent passage to Quebec aboard the SS *Montrose*. The cellar was dug up. Hyoscine was found in the viscera and an abdominal scar went towards identification. Le Neve, tried on her own, was acquitted. Crippen (born in 1862) was hanged at Pentonville Prison on November 23rd, 1910.

Prime sources: *Notable British Trial,* edited by Filson Young, William Hodge, Edinburgh, 1920.
Doctor Crippen, Max Constantine Quinn, Duckworth, London, 1935.
Dr. Crippen, Michael Gilbert, Odhams Press, London, 1953.
Crippen: The Mild Murderer, Tom Cullen, The Bodley Head, London, 1977.
The Crippen File, Jonathan Goodman, Allison & Busby, London, 1985.

58

Albert Henry DeSalvo

The Boston Strangler

Serial killer

Murderer: Albert Henry DeSalvo.
Victims: 13 women, aged 19-85. Anna Slesers, Mary
Mullen, Nina Nichols, Helen Blake, Ida Irga, Jane
Sullivan, Sophie Clark, Patricia Bissette, Mary Brown,
Beverly Samans, Evelyn Corbin, Joann Graff, Mary
Sullivan.
Loci: Boston, Lynn, Salem, Cambridge and Lawrence,
USA.
Dates: June 1962 – January 1964.
Means: Strangulation with a ligature, typically
stockings. Some variations: knifing, battering, manual
strangulation.
Motive: A continuum of sexual gratification, with rape
usually before the murder, although there may have
been some blurring of the sequence.
Crimewatch: DeSalvo was never tried for the stranglings.
He was protected by his status as an insane person, when
he confessed in convincing detail to the Boston murders.
At that time, he was an inmate at Bridgewater State
Hospital, judged unfit to stand trial for a series of sexual
assaults in his other personae as 'The Measuring Man'
and 'The Green Man', by reason of schizophrenia, of
which there is precious little published evidence. Finally
sentenced to life imprisonment on the lesser charges,
aged 36, he was found, on November 26th, 1973,
stabbed to death, the only occupant of the hospital block
at Walpole State Prison, Massachusetts.

Prime sources: *The Boston Strangler,* Gerold Frank, The New
American Library, New York, 1966.
The Strangler: The Story of Terror in Boston, Harold K. Banks,
Mayflower Paperbacks, London, 1967.
The Official Tape-Recorded Confessions of the Boston Strangler,
edited by George W. Rae, Tandem-Ortolan, London, 1967.

Jeannie Ewen or Donald

The Aberdeen Sack Murder

Murderer: Jeannie Ewen or Donald.
Victim: Helen Wilson Robertson Priestly (8½).
Locus: 61 Urquhart Road, Aberdeen.
Date: April 20th, 1934.
Means: Asphyxia. Most likely due to inhalation of vomit. But possibly strangulation.
Motive: Never discovered..
Crimewatch: Helen, aged 8½, was sent to buy a loaf. She never returned. At 5 a.m. next day her violated body was found in a sack at the foot of her tenement stair. Her injuries simulated rape. Special theory: The child used to taunt 38-year-old Mrs. Donald, calling her 'Coconut' and ringing her bell. Mrs. Donald caught her and gave her a good shaking. Helen, who had an enlarged thymus gland, passed into deep, deathlike unconsciousness. Thinking she had killed her, Mrs. Donald made it look like a male sexual attack. Sentenced to death, but respited to life, she was released in 1944.

Prime source: *Notable British Trial,* edited by John G. Wilson, William Hodge, Edinburgh, 1953.

Samuel Herbert Dougal

The Moat Farm Murder

Murderer: Samuel Herbert Dougal.
Victim: Camille Cecille Holland (56).
Locus: Moat Farm, Clavering, Essex.
Date: May 19th, 1899.
Means: Shooting in the head with a revolver.
Motive: Financial gain: for four years, until the murder was discovered, 'Captain' Dougal, (born in 1846), adventurer and philanderer, forged Miss Holland's signature in order to milk her financial assets.
Crimewatch: Lured to the lonely love-nest, Miss Holland survived only three weeks before Dougal struck. Her body lay hidden in a drainage ditch, covered and preserved by blackthorn bushes until it was dug out on April 27th, 1903. And while Camille reclined amid the blackthorns, the gallant Captain amused himself by training nude girl bicyclists in the Moat Farm field. He was hanged on July 14th, 1903, at Chelmsford Prison.

Prime source: *Notable British Trial,* edited by F. Tennyson Jesse, William Hodge, Edinburgh, 1928.

Elizabeth Diane Frederickson Downs

Murderer: Elizabeth Diane Frederickson Downs.
Victim: Cheryl Lynn Downs (7): daughter.
Locus: Old Mohawk Road, near Springfield, Oregon.
Date: May 19th, 1983.
Means: Two .22 bullets in the back.
Motive: Theoretical only: no confession. Could have been more psychologically complex, or more frankly disordered, than the State's construct that Diane Downs, who was divorced, tried to eliminate all three of her children because her married, and luke-warm, lover, Lewis Lewiston, 'never wanted kids – or to be a father.'
Crimewatch: Diane Downs (27) blamed the ubiquitous Bushy-haired Stranger for the gun attack which also left Christie (8) and Danny (3) permanently impaired. Assistant DA Fred Hugi later took the two survivors into his own home. Christie had recovered sufficiently to give evidence against her mother. The gun, a .22 semi-automatic Luger, numbered 14-57485, was not found. Immeasurably disturbed, Diane Downs gave a history of sexual abuse by her own father. Even so, she had given birth to a child under a surrogacy scheme. Sentenced to life imprisonment, she escaped from Oregon Women's Correctional Centre, and was transferred to Clinton, New Jersey, with no hope of parole until 2014.

Prime source: *Small Sacrifices*, Ann Rule, New American Library, 1987.

William Henry Theodore Durrant

The Girl in the Belfry Murder

Murderer: William Henry Theodore Durrant.
Victims: Blanche Lamont (21). Minnie Williams (20).
Locus: Emanuel Baptist Church, Bartlett Street, San Francisco.
Dates: April 3rd, 1895 (Lamont). April 12th, 1895 (Williams).
Means: Manual strangulation (Lamont). Suffocation, with pieces of victim's own dress, and stabbings (Williams).
Motive: No certainty here. Sex enters. Frustration at rejection by Blanche Lamont is the most popular reconstruction. Frenzy is attached to the murder of Minnie Williams. Possibly she knew too much of the first murder.
Crimewatch: Durrant (24) was a young man of good character, a medical student and an assistant superintendent of the Sunday School at the Emanuel Baptist Church. His sister was Maud Allan, the dancer. His mental disturbance unguessed at, he dragged Blanche's body up to the bell-less belfry, where she lay nude and white, indeed marmoreal, until discovery. Minnie was despatched gorily in the church library, her body stowed in a closet. Ridiculous rumours, such as the implication of the pastor, encrusted the case. Durrant was hanged at San Quentin on January 7th, 1898. 'Papa,' his mother is supposed to have said to Durrant's father as refreshment was fetched to the grieving parents, three feet from their son's cut-down corpse in its coffin, 'I'll take some more of that roast.'

Prime source: *The Girl in the Belfry,* Joseph Henry Jackson and Lenore Glen Offord, Gold Medal Books, Fawcett Publications, Greenwich, Connecticut, 1957.

Ruth Ellis

Murderer: Ruth Ellis.

Victim: David Blakely (25).

Locus: Outside the Magdala public-house, at the foot of South Hill Park, Hampstead, London.

Date: April 10th, 1955.

Means: Shooting with a .38 calibre six-shot Smith & Wesson revolver.

Motive: A crime of passion, of course. Ruth Ellis killed the thing she loved. There was sexual jealousy and rage at violent ill-treatment by her lover, a racing driver.

Crimewatch: Ruth Ellis, born October 9th, 1926, was the last woman to be hanged in Britain – on July 13th, 1955, at Holloway Prison. Her case went towards the abolition of hanging. She had suffered a miscarriage very recently – on March 28th. It is thought that her distraught state of mind would have come under the Diminished Responsibility defence which reduces murder to manslaughter – but that was not enacted until the Homicide Act 1957. A defence of provocation had failed at the trial, because of the arguable degree of premeditation. Appeal failed. If a shot had not ricocheted and wounded the hand of an innocent bystander, Mrs. Gladys Yule, Ruth Ellis might have been spared.

Prime sources: *Ruth Ellis,* Robert Hancock, Arthur Barker, London, 1963.
The Trial of Ruth Ellis, Jonathan Goodman and Patrick Pringle, Celebrated Trials Series, David & Charles, Newton Abbot, Devon, 1974.
Ruth Ellis: A Case of Diminished Responsibility? Laurence Marks and Tony Van den Bergh, Macdonald and Jane's, London, 1977.

Marie Marguerite Fahmy

The Savoy Hotel Murder

Accused: Marie Marguerite Fahmy.
Victim: Prince Ali Kamel Fahmy Bey: husband (22).
He was not, in fact, a prince, but a bey.
Locus: Suite No. 41, on the fourth floor of the Savoy
Hotel, The Strand, London.
Date: July 10th, 1923.
Means: Shooting with a .32 Browning semi
automatic pistol.
Motive: Impulsive elimination of a threatening and
oppressive figure.
Crimewatch: Of humble origin, daughter of a
Parisian cab driver and a charwoman, Marie
Marguerite Alibert had ascended via prostitution and
courtesanship to good position and considerable
personal affluence. Motivated by avarice, she married
spectacularly wealthy Prince Fahmy, aged 22 – ten
years her junior. There was a six-month history of
severe marital disharmony; threats and physical
violence. Marguerite Fahmy shot her husband in hot
blood during a violent thunderstorm. Defence by
Marshall Hall, unashamedly racial, presented
Madame Fahmy as the alleged victim of oriental
cruelty and the unnatural sexual practices of a
vengeful bisexual husband. A sympathetic occidental
jury acquitted her.

Prime source: *Scandal at the Savoy,* Andrew Rose,
Bloomsbury, London, 1991.

Albert Howard Fish

Serial killer

Murderer: Albert Howard Fish.
Victims: Murdered at least 15 children.
Loci: Grace Budd, aged 12, was murdered at
Wisteria Cottage, Irvington, Westchester County,
New York, and other unidentified children all over
America.
Dates: June 3rd, 1928 (Grace Budd). Others over a
period of years up to his arrest in 1934.
Means: Strangulation, knifing and other horrors
unguessed at.
Motive: Sexual satisfaction in a grossly deviant
personality. Cannibalism was the dominant drive,
with antecedent sado masochistic acts. There was a
strong family history of mental illness.
Crimewatch: Decidedly elderly for a serial killer,
stooped, seamed house-painter Fish (born May 19th,
1870), was captured six years after he had slain and
eaten what he fancied of Grace Budd in isolated
Wisteria Cottage. Good detective work traced him to
200 East 52nd Street, New York City, through his use
of a printed envelope to enclose a taunting
descriptive letter to Grace Budd's mother. A product
of an orphanage, where he had become
coprophagous, he had been married, with six
children, but for years had been mastered by his
sado-masochistic urges. At least a hundred serious
sadistic acts on children, not amounting to actual
murder, are attributed to Fish. He would pounce
upon his victims in the nude. Sometimes his painter's
overall would carry ambiguous red splashes. In his
own words, 'I learned to like the taste of human flesh

many years ago during a famine in China. It is something like veal. Little girls have more flavour than little boys.' A routine X-ray disclosed 29 separate needles which Fish had inserted into the skin around his testicles. He looked forward to his electrocution at Sing Sing on January 16th, 1936, as the ultimate thrill. He helped the executioner to attach the electrodes to his leg. The first charge of electricity failed, perhaps short-circuited by his cache of needles.

Prime sources: *Trail of Blood,* Michael Angelella, Bobbs-Merrill, Indianapolis/New York, 1979.
Deranged, Harold Schechter, Pocket Books, New York, 1990.

Sidney Harry Fox

The Margate Matricide

Murderer: Sidney Harry Fox.

Victim: Rosaline Fox (63): mother.

Locus: Room 66, Hotel Metropole, Paradise Street, Margate, Kent.

Date: October 23rd, 1929.

Means: Strangulation.

Motive: Financial gain from life insurance policies.

Crimewatch: Convicted conman and forger, Sidney Fox, (born January, 1899), aping his betters, lived by the skin of his teeth, bilking hoteliers. His silver-haired mother tottered along with him, a part of his stock-in-trade. Their only luggage was a brown paper parcel. Even Mother was expendable. To cash in, Fox had to show that she had died by accident before the midnight of October 23rd. After he had despatched her on the bed, he lit a fire under a chair, and when the smoke was dense, called the alarm at 11.40 p.m. Sir Bernard Spilsbury alone discerned a small bruise on the larynx indicative of strangulation. The hyoid bone, unusually but not uniquely, was intact. Sidney Fox was hanged at Maidstone Gaol on April 8th, 1930.

Prime source: *Notable British Trial*, edited by F. Tennyson Jesse, William Hodge, Edinburgh, 1934.

Augusta Fairfield Fullam

The Agra Double Murder

Henry Lovell William Clark

Murderers: Augusta Fairfield Fullam. Henry Lovell William Clark.

Victims: Edward McKeon Fullam (44): husband. Louisa Amelia Clark (c. 55): wife.

Loci: 9 Metcalfe Road, Agra, India (Mr. Fullam). 135 Cantonments, Agra, India (Mrs. Clark).

Dates: October 10th, 1911 (Fullam). November 17th, 1912 (Clark).

Means: Poisoning by arsenic, finally, probably by gelsemine and cocaine (Fullam). Procured slaying by assassins with sword-slashes to the head (Clark).

Motive: Freedom from matrimony so that the surviving partners could marry each other.

Crimewatch: Augusta, daughter of a Bengal river pilot, minor memsahib of the British Raj, a tubby temptress with claws of steel, shockingly fell in love with half-Indian Dr. Clark (born August 15th, 1868). Before they met, he had already tried to poison his wife, Louisa, and it was he who instigated the double murder plan, which Augusta enthusiastically embraced. Unwisely, she kept in a trunk her own incriminating letters to Clark in which she discussed the slow poisoning of her husband by packets of arsenic masked as 'tonic powders' sent by post to her by Clark. Louisa was tougher, more 'poison-proof' than Eddie Fullam, and the murderous pair had recourse to the bazaars of Agra for the recruitment of a band of 'badmashes', who killed Louisa in her bed while Clark was absent setting up a false alibi. Upon interrogation, he fluffed and fumbled the details of that alibi. The trunk of letters was found. Augusta and Clark were tried jointly at Allahabad High Court in 1913. Both were found guilty and sentenced to death. Clark was hanged on March 26th, 1913, but Augusta's sentence was commuted to penal servitude for life, because she was pregnant by Clark. A son was born in prison. He survived and lived a good life, but Augusta died of heatstroke in Naini Prison, aged 38, on May 28th, 1914. The assassins were tried separately: three were hanged, one got off on alibi.

Prime sources: *The Agra Double Murder,* Sir Cecil Walsh, Ernest Benn, London, 1929.
Khaki Mischief, Molly Whittington – Egan, Souvenir Press, London, 1990.

John Wayne Gacy

The Killer Clown

Serial killer

Murderer: John Wayne Gacy.
Victims: 33 boys and young men.
Locus: 8213 Summerdale Avenue, Norwood Park Township, Chicago.
Dates: 1972-78.
Means: Strangulation.
Motive: Sexual gratification. Sadistic sodomitic rape, with beating and whipping.
Crimewatch: Gacy, born March 17th, 1942, who had a long history of sexual perversion, loved to attend children's parties dressed as a clown. He stowed victims' bodies in the crawl space under his house and in the garden, and dumped extra ones in rivers. At his emotional trial, the Prosecution placed photographs of 22 identified victims on a ten-foot high wooden board facing the jury. Paramedics stood by to attend weeping relatives. Sentenced on March 13th, 1980, to the electric chair, Gacy survived on Death Row, Stateville Correctional Centre, through the process of appeals. On April 8th, 1991, a judge scheduled a hearing on a writ of Federal habeas corpus which argued constitutional errors in the trial.

Prime sources: *The Man Who Killed Boys,* Clifford L. Linedecker, St. Martin's Press, New York, 1980.
Killer Clown, Terry Sullivan with Peter T. Maiken, Grosset & Dunlap, New York, 1983.
Buried Dreams, Tim Cahill, Bantam Books, New York, 1986.

Gerald Armond Gallego alias Feil

Serial killer

Murderer: Gerald Armond Gallego.
Victims: Rhonda Scheffler (17). Kippi Vaught (14).
Brenda Judd (15). Sandra Kaye Colley (14). Stacy
Ann Redican (17). Karen Chipman-Twiggs (17).
Linda Teresa Aguilar (21). Virginia Mochel (34).
Craig Raymond Miller (22). Mary Beth Sowers (21).
Loci: Near Baxter, 15 miles east of Sacramento,
California (Scheffler and Vaught). Somewhere in the
vicinity of Reno, Nevada, but bodies never found
(Judd and Colley). Near Lovelock, Nevada (Redican
and Chipman-Twiggs). Some nine miles south of
Gold Beach, Oregon (Aguilar). Skeletal remains near
Sacramento, California (Mochel). Remote spot near
Bass Lake Road, Eldorado County, California
(Miller). Cow pasture somewhere between Rocklin
and Loomis, north-east of Sacramento, California
(Sowers).
Dates: September 11th, 1978 (Scheffler and
Vaught). June 24th, 1979 (Judd and Colley). April
24th, 1980 (Redican and Chipman-Twiggs). June
16th, 1980 (Aguilar). July 17th, 1980 (Mochel).
November 1st-2nd, 1980 (Miller and Sowers).
Means: Shooting, bludgeoning to death. Aguilar,
after being beaten severely about the head with a
hammer, was buried alive.
Motive: All sexually motivated killings except in the
case of Miller who had to be killed because he
happened to be in the company of the victim.
Crimewatch: Born in 1947, son of a three-times
killer who had been despatched in the Mississippi gas
chamber at the age of 28. Seven times married, twice

to the same woman, Gallego, a Sacramento, California, nightclub bartender, had been sodomising and sexually abusing his own daughter since she was six. Pursuing a compulsive fantasy, he sought the perfect lover and sex-slave. In fact, he had found her in his wife, Charlene, who, acting as pander, lured young girls picked up in such places as the Sacramento shopping mall, into his van with promises of marijuana. She would sit complacently in the front, while on a crude bed in the back of the van her satyriasic husband ravaged and savaged and killed his victims. She then helped to bury them. The Gallegos were caught after a friend of their last victim's managed to jot down the number of the kidnap car. In a plea-bargaining deal which gave her a 16-year prison sentence plus immunity from any further prosecution, Charlene finally agreed to testify against her husband. Twice tried – in California and Nevada respectively – twice condemned to die, Gallego awaits execution.

Prime source: *All His Father's Sins*, Lt. Ray Biondi and Walt Hecox, Prima Publishing, Rocklin, California, 1988.

William George Last Gardiner

The Peasenhall Murder

Accused: William George Last Gardiner.
Victim: Rose Harsent (23).
Locus: Providence House, Rendham Hill,
Peasenhall, Saxmundham, Suffolk.
Date: May 31st – 1st June, 1902.
Means: Throat cut.
Motive: Elimination of inconveniently pregnant girl.
Crimewatch: Bucolic crime in turn-of-the-century
primitive village community. Sex and incest behind
the innocent hedgerows. Gardiner, Methodist Elder,
Sunday School Superintendent, 36-year-old father of
six, accused of sexual dalliance with 23-year-old Rose,
servant at Providence House, was charged with her
murder. After two juries disagreed, the Crown lodged
a *nolle prosequi*. Gardiner, who moved to Southall,
Middlesex, and took over a grocer's shop, has
traditionally been held to have been fortunate, but
latest research, based on the comparison of
Gardiner's handwriting with that of an unsigned
assignation note sent to Rose on the day of the
murder, is held by some to go towards Gardiner's
innocence.

Prime sources: *Notable British Trial*, edited by William
Henderson, William Hodge, Edinburgh, 1934.
The Peasenhall Mystery, John Rowland, John Long, London,
1962.
The Peasenhall Murder, Edwin Packer, Yoxford Publications,
Saxmundham, Suffolk, 1980.
The Peasenhall Murder, Martin Fido and Keith Skinner, Alan
Sutton, Stroud, Gloucestershire, 1990.

Edward Theodore Gein

The original of Hitchcock's *Psycho*

Probable Serial killer

Murderer: Edward Theodore Gein.
Victims: Mary Hogan (51). Bernice Worden (58). Quite probably others.
Locus: Gein farm, near Plainfield, Waushara, Wisconsin.
Dates: December 8th, 1954 (Hogan). November 16th, 1957 (Worden).
Means: Shooting with a Mauser pistol (Hogan) and a rifle (Worden).
Motive: Sexual and emotional gratification, with disordered thinking.
Crimewatch: It was Mother who screwed up young Eddie. Augusta Gein (pronounced 'Geen') reared him to have nothing to do with women. But he was very, very interested in them. And when Augusta died, and he was 39, he nailed up her room and went out to the graveyards to dig himself up some women to play with. About nine of them. He did not like their smell, and the murders were a natural extension of his activities. The decapitated body of Mrs. Worden, his last victim, was found hanging by the heels from a crossbar hoisted by a block and tackle in a shed at the neglected Gein farm. The body was gutted and dressed out like a deer from the local woods. Dark rooms held more secrets: skulls on the bedposts, a belt of nipples, bowls made from skull-caps, a wastepaper basket, lampshades and chair-seats made out of human skin, a knife-handle of human bone, a shade-pull with a pair of woman's lips attached, skin puttees, nine vulvas in a shoe-box (one trimmed with red ribbon), four noses, Mary

Hogan's mask of skin and hair, nine more masks,
Mrs. Worden's head, with bent nails ready as hooks in
the ears, and her heart in a sauccpan on the stove.
There was the skin of a woman's torso, with breasts,
stiff and tanned like leather. Gein admitted that he
used to tie it on and, with a real-face mask and with a
vulva or two tied on to his genitalia, dance in the yard
in the moonlight. He kept the skin nicely oiled.
Three graves were opened to check Gein's
confession. They were, indeed, empty or violated. He
was incarcerated as insane through schizophrenia
(although he instructed Counsel remarkably well),
died at Mendota Institute, aged 78, and was interred
beside Mother. He took with him a ghastly mystery:
two of his collection of vulvas were judged to have
come from girls of about fifteen, but the records of
local cemeteries showed that no girls aged 12 to 18
had been buried there during Gein's time. So there
must have been two more live victims.

Prime sources: *Edward Gein: America's Most Bizarre Murderer,*
Judge Robert H. Gollmar, Chas. Hallberg, Delavan,
Wisconsin, 1982.
Deviant, Harold Schechter, Pocket Books, New York, 1989.

Harvey Murray Glatman

Serial killer

Murderer: Harvey Murray Glatman.
Victims: Judy Ann Van Horn Dull (19). Shirley Ann
Loy Bridgeford (24). Ruth Rita Mercado (24).
Loci: Beside the highway, in the desert, near Indio,
California (Dull). Beside Butterfield Stage Road,
Anza Borrego, Desert State Park, California
(Bridgeford and Mercado).
Dates: August 1st, 1957 – around midnight (Dull).
March 9th, 1958 (Bridgeford). July 24th, 1958
(Mercado).
Means: Strangulation from behind. Victim so
trussed and bent backwards that the cord securing
ʇɥǝ ɐnᴉɯɐʅ ⱳɐⱯ ʅǝɓs ɐʅₛₒ ₐcₜₑd ₐₛ ₐ gₐᵣᵣₒₜₑ.
Motive: Rape – followed by disposal to avoid
identification.
Crimewatch: Jug-eared Glatman (born 1928),
unattractive to women, had given up normal
methods of approach. For robbing women, in which
connection he was known as 'The Phantom Bandit',
he had already been sentenced to five years in Sing
Sing. He did not like prison. Posing as a professional
photographer, while really a television repair man,
brought him closer to the good-lookers who would
otherwise have scorned him. In the desert he tied
them up (he had a thing about ropes) and raped and
photographed them, right up to the end. That was
the extent of his perversions. Dull and Mercado were
models, but he got hold of Bridgeford through a
dating agency. Dangerous. If his next potential
victim, model Lorraine Vigil (27), had not fought
back and grabbed his gun, a Belgian Browning, he

might have continued his course for years. A Highway patrolman came to her rescue when he saw the couple wrestling in the sand. Photographs of the three dead girls – and a collection of ropes – were found in Glatman's sordid Los Angeles bungalow at 1011 South Norton Avenue. He confessed, pleaded guilty, and was despatched in the San Quentin gas chamber on September 18th, 1959. No doubt there are some photographs, somewhere.

Prime source: Contemporary newspapers.

Identity unknown

The Green River Killer

William Jay Stevens

Serial killer

Murderer: Identity unknown.
Victims: Accredited with the slaying of at least 49 women and one unborn child. Mary Bridget Meehan (18) was eight months pregnant.
Loci: Victims mainly picked up on the 'Sea-Tac Strip' highway, running south from Seattle to Tacoma. First five corpses found in and beside the Green River, Washington State. Thereafter, skeletal remains found in various locations, Washington State.
Dates: July 1982 – March 1984.
Means: Strangling in the cases of the first five victims discovered – Deborah Lynn Bonner (22) Wendy Coffield (16). Marcia Faye Chapman (31). Cynthia Hinds (17). Opal Mills (16). Thereafter such was the condition of the remains – mere heaps of bones – that death by homicidal violence was the only possible assignable reason.
Motive: Unascertainable with any precision, but very likely to be sexually oriented.
Crimewatch: The series began officially on August 12th, 1982, with the discovery of the naked body of Deborah Bonner in the Green River, near a slaughterhouse in Kent, King County, Washington State, although, a month earlier and not half a mile away, the body of Wendy Coffield had been found in the Green River. In the next couple of years the body-count reached 49. The victims were mainly prostitutes and teenage runaways scooped up from the sleazy, sex-for-sale, Sea-Tac Strip, driven to some secluded spot in the woods and strangled. The killer

left no clues. There were, however, two main suspects: Melvyn Wayne Foster, a 44-year-old taxicab driver who seemed to know too much, arrested in September 1982, but subsequently cleared, and William J. Stevens II (38), a third-year law student at Gonzaga University, Spokane. Stevens had photographs of nude women, a collection of police badges and uniforms, and an expressed fascination with Ted Bundy. But it was announced by Captain Bob Evans of the Green River Task Force that, "We have come to the conclusion that we can no longer call him a viable suspect."

Prime source: *The Search for the Green River Killer,* Carlton Smith and Tomas Guillen, Onyx Books, New York, 1991.

John George Haigh

The Acid Bath Murders

Mass murderer

Murderer: John George Haigh.
Victims: William Donald McSwan (34). Donald McSwan (70) and his wife, Amy McSwan (65). Dr. Archibald Henderson (52) and his wife, Rosalie Henderson (41). Mrs. Olive Henrietta Helen Olivia Robarts Durand-Deacon (69). Haigh confessed to nine murders in all. Three remain unknown and were probably apocryphal.
Loci: The McSwans in the basement of 79 Gloucester Road, Kensington, London, S.W.7. The Hendersons and Mrs. Durand-Deacon in a storehouse belonging to Hurstlea Products, Ltd., in Giles Yard, Leopold Road, on the outskirts of Crawley, Sussex.
Dates: William Donald McSwan. September 9th, 1944. Donald and Amy McSwan. *c.* July 2nd, 1945. Dr. Archibald and Rosalie Henderson *c.* February 13th, 1948. Mrs. Durand-Deacon, February 18th, 1949.
Means: Shooting in the cases of the Hendersons and Mrs. Durand-Deacon. The McSwans were most probably killed by blows to the head.
Motive: The purest of all motives – Money.
Crimewatch: Pretending interest in commercial idea of Mrs. Durand-Deacon, fellow guest at the Onslow Court Hotel, Queen's Gate, South Kensington, of manufacturing plastic finger-nails, Haigh drove her to Crawley, shot her and, pausing briefly to eat an egg on toast at Ye Anciente Priory Restaurant, dissolved her body in a drum of sulphuric acid before going off to dine at the George Hotel. Bone fragments, gallstones and an undissolved acrylic

plastic denture in the resultant sludge led to his arrest. Hazarding an insanity defence, he claimed to have drunk his victims' blood. Vampiric plea rejected, he was hanged, aged 40, at Wandsworth Prison on August 10th, 1949.

Prime sources: *Notable British Trial,* edited by Lord Dunboyne, William Hodge, Edinburgh, 1953.
Haigh: The Mind of a Murderer, Arthur La Bern, W. H. Allen, London, 1973.
The Acid Bath Murders, David Briffett, Field Place Press, Broadbridge Heath, West Sussex, 1988.

Archibald Thomson Hall alias Roy Fontaine

The Monster Butler Mass murderer

Murderer: Archibald Thomson Hall.
Victims: David Wright (30): blackmailer of the butler. Dorothy Alice Scott-Elliot (60): wife of employer. Walter Travers Scott-Elliot (82): employer. Mary Coggle (51): accomplice to murder of the Scott-Elliots. Donald Hall (36): brother of the butler.
Loci: Woodland by Kirtleton Hall, near Waterbeck, Dumfriesshire (Wright). 22 Richmond Court, Sloane Street, Chelsea, London (Dorothy Scott-Elliot). Glen Affric, Inverness-shire (Walter Scott-Elliot). Middle Farm Cottage, Newton Arlosh, Cumbria (Coggle and Hall).
Dates.   August/September 1977 (Wright). December 8th, 1977 (Dorothy Scott-Elliot). December 14th, 1977 (Walter Scott-Elliot). December 17th, 1977 (Coggle). January 1st, 1978 (Hall).
Means: Shooting with a .22 rifle (Wright). Suffocation with a pillow (Dorothy Scott-Elliot). Strangling and hitting with a spade (Walter Scott-Elliot). Battering with a poker (Coggle). Chloroform (Hall).
Motive: Broadly, financial gain, and the concealment thereof. Finally, the concealment of those murders themselves.
Crimewatch: The monster butler was a conman and a jewel thief. He was good at his job. First, he shot Wright, blackmailer from prison days, who threatened to expose him. Next, the butler killed Scott-Elliot, ex-MP, and his wife, in pursuit of their antiques and assets. By now he had two accomplices,

Michael Kitto (39) and Mary Coggle. The butler got rid of Coggle because she refused to relinquish Mrs. Scott-Elliot's incriminating mink coat. Finally, so deep in blood that he could not draw back, the butler silenced his own brother, another weak link and a liability. After hearings at the Edinburgh High Court and the Old Bailey, both Hall (born July 17th, 1924) and Kitto were sentenced to life imprisonment.

Prime sources: *The Monster Butler,* Norman Lucas and Philip Davies, Arthur Barker, London, 1979.
The Butler, James Copeland, Panther Books, 1981, London.

James Hanratty

Murderer: James Hanratty.
Victim: Michael Gregsten (*c.* 36). Married lover of Valerie Storie. (23).
Locus: A lay-by off the A6, at the top of Deadman's Hill, near Ampthill, Bedfordshire.
Date: August 23rd, 1961.
Means: Two shots from a .38 Enfield revolver.
Motive: Probably a panic reaction.
Crimewatch: Man approached Gregsten and Storie, love-making, *circa* 9 p.m., in car parked in remote cornfield, at Dorney Reach, near Maidenhead, Berkshire. He forced Gregsten at gunpoint to drive to Bedfordshire, shot him dead, raped Miss Storie, then shot and paralysed her. Hanratty was arrested Claimed conflicting Liverpool and Rhyl alibis. Peter Louis Alphon confessed to the killing, triggering a controversy still raging long after 25-year-old Hanratty's hanging at Bedford on April 4th, 1962. Issue complicated by the weird circumstance that both Hanratty and Alphon had stayed in the seedy Vienna Hotel, Maida Vale, London, where two cartridges from the A6 murder gun were found. The *full* story of how and why the killer came to be in the cornfield is still to be told.

Prime sources: *The A6 Murder,* Louis Blom-Cooper, Penguin Books, London, 1963.
Murder vs. Murder, Jean Justice, Olympia Press, Paris, 1964.
Deadman's Hill: Was Hanratty Guilty? Lord Russell, Secker & Warburg, London, 1965.
Who Killed Hanratty? Paul Foot, Jonathan Cape, London, 1971.
The Case of James Hanratty, Report of Mr. C. Lewis Hawser, Q.C., HMSO, April 1975, Cmnd. 6021.

Neville George Clevely Heath

Murderer: Neville George Clevely Heath alias Group Captain Rupert Brooke.

Victims: Margery Aimee Brownell Gardner (32). Doreen Marshall (21).

Loci: Room 4, Pembridge Court Hotel, 34 Pembridge Gardens, London, W.2. (Gardner). Branksome Dene Chine, Bournemouth (Marshall).

Dates: June 21st, 1946 (Gardner). July 4th, 1946 (Marshall).

Means: Suffocation, with beating with a riding whip and sexual mutilations inflicted ante mortem (Gardner). The throat was cut, with sexual mutilations inflicted post mortem. (Marshall).

Motive: Sexual gratification.

Crimewatch: A sado-masochistic encounter in Room 4, with bondage and flagellation, went wrong: apparently there had been previous such transactions. In the alternative, Heath (29) had intended the worst. When he saw what he had done, he thirsted for more. Doreen Marshall, *not* a masochist, was enticeable and he did as he pleased with her in the bushes of the gladsome resort. His defence of insanity was doomed to failure, and it was an incorrigible psychopath that they hanged at Pentonville on October 26th, 1946.

Prime sources: *Notable British Trial*, edited by Macdonald Critchley, William Hodge, Edinburgh, 1951.
Borstal Boy: The Uncensored Story of Neville Heath, Gerald Byrne, John Hill Productions, London, nd.
Portrait of a Sadist, Paull Hill, Neville Spearman, London, 1960.
Rotten to the Core? Francis Selwyn, Routledge, London, 1988.

Gary Heidnik

Set on course for a serial killer

Murderer: Gary Heidnik.
Victims: The dead: Sandra Lindsay (25). Deborah
Johnson Dudley (23). Prisoners: Josefina Rivera (26).
Lisa Thomas (19). Jacquelyn Askins (18). Agnes
Adams (24).
Locus: 3520 North Marshall Street, Philadelphia.
Dates: November 26th, 1986: Josefina Rivera picked
up. November 29th, 1986: Sandra Lindsay captured.
December 22nd, 1986: Lisa Thomas imprisoned.
January 1st, 1987: Deborah Johnson Dudley
captured. January 18th, 1987: Jacquelyn Askins
kidnapped. March 23rd, 1987: Agnes Adams
captured.
Means: Sandra Lindsay, after dangling by one wrist
from an overhead beam for a week, choked to death
on a lump of bread forced down her throat. Deborah
Dudley was electrocuted – by a live wire lowered into
the water-filled pit in the cellar into which Heidnik
had put her.
Motive: Who knows? To punish insubordination on
the part of sex slaves? *Pour encourager les autres?* We
are in muddied psychiatric waters here.
Crimewatch: Legally, Heidnik was not insane. By no
stretch of the imagination, however, could he be
proposed as a personification of normalcy. His I.Q.
was high – 130-148 on various testings – yet he
deliberately elected intimacy with severely mentally
retarded black women. He had considerable flare for
investment and by its shrewd deployment was
possessed of more than half a million dollars – yet
chose to live meagrely and filthily in a black slum. He
indulged strangely conflicting fancies. He founded

the United Church of the Ministers of God – and it was not wholly a scam. The stock market apart, his main interests – hobbies, really – were pornography, black prostitutes and top-class cars. He had a plan to start his own baby farm in the basement, and went out hunting black girls to bear his children. He kept them chained and shackled prisoners. He killed two. He fed the survivors on dog meat mixed with the minced flesh of his victim (Lindsay), kept them in a black pit, and drove screwdrivers down their ears. He was captured after a captive (Rivera) managed to slip out of his clutches and led incredulous police to his church-cum-torture-house. Convicted of two first-degree murders, he is scheduled for the electric chair.

Prime source: *Cellar of Horror,* Ken Englade, Angus & Robertson, London, 1989.

Elbert Ervin Homan

Murderer: Elbert Ervin Homan.
Victim: William List (57).
Locus: Todville Road, Seabrook, Texas.
Date: October 17th, 1984.
Means: Shotgun.
Motive: Scrawled on the wall above wreckage wrought to List's luxury home – chandeliers smashed, furniture broken and scattered with food on the floor, acid poured into the Jacuzzi, a 50,000-dollar crystal water fountain reduced to smithereens – 'No more pain. Bill List is a sick man. No more fist for List. Have a nice day.'
Crimewatch: Homan, born December 23rd, 1965, started off in life with big ambitions. He dreamt of becoming a lawyer or a policeman. The son of divorced parents, his unstable background undoubtedly contributed to his status as a troublemaker at school. He graduated to a street-wise life via the Covenant House, a Houston, Texas, home for runaways and street kids. Life became an up and down affair of drug-induced highs and desperate shifts-for-a-living lows. The pseudo-glamour of Westheimer Boulevard hooked him. October 13th, 1984, standing outside a Westheimer grocery store, Homan was picked up by homosexual oil rig trailer maker, multimillionaire, William List. He took the teenager to his 30-room mansion and invited him to live there with him and three other youngsters. Here was undreamt of luxury and Bill was generous with drugs. But, as always in life, there was a price to be paid. Bill's 'guests' were forced to strip nude and submit to torture. They were required also to

minister to List's highly weird anal erotic needs.
Enough for him was more than enough for his
houseguests. Homan freed them all from List's tacky
embraces – by sacrificing his own freedom for 45
years.

Prime source: Contemporary newspapers.

Brian Donald Hume alias Donald Brown, John Stephen Bird

Murderer: Brian Donald Hume aka Donald Brown, John Stephen Bird.

Victims: Stanley Setty aka Sulman Seti (46). Arthur Maag (50).

Loci: 620 Finchley Road, Golders Green, London (Setty). Zurich (Maag).

Dates: October 4th, 1949 (Setty). January 30th, 1959 (Maag).

Means: Stabbing with German S.S. dagger (Setty). Shooting with Manhurin 7.65 mm pistol (Maag).

Motive: Spur of the moment quarrel – with incidental financial gain (Setty). Attempting to evade capture (Maag).

Crimewatch: Clever, calculating, cold, psychopath. Tried for the murder of his spivvish criminal partner, Setty, whose corpse, after dismemberment, he dropped piecemeal from an aircraft into the English Channel. The jury disagreed. Hume pleaded guilty to second indictment as accessory after the fact. Sentenced to 12 years. Released February 1958. Sold confession of guilt to *Sunday Pictorial.* Returned to a life of escalating crime and violence, in January 1959, Hume killed again, while robbing the Gewerbe Bank, Ramistrasse, Zurich. Sentenced by Swiss court to life imprisonment. His victim, Arthur Maag, a taxi driver, who unwisely "had a go". Brought back to England and Broadmoor in 1976. Transferred in 1988, aged 69, to St. Bernard's Psychiatric Hospital, Southall, Middlesex.

Prime sources: *Hume: Portrait of a Double Killer,* John Williams, Heinemann, London, 1960.
Trials of Brian Donald Hume, Ivan Butler, David & Charles, Newton Abbot, Devon, 1976.

Jack the Ripper

Serial killer

Elizabeth Stride

Murderer: Jack the Ripper. Unidentified.
Victims: Mary Ann Nichols (42-45). Annie Chapman (47). Elizabeth Stride (44-45). Catherine Eddowes (43). Mary Jane Kelly (25).
Loci: Buck's Row, Whitechapel (Nichols). Backyard of 29 Hanbury Street, Spitalfields (Chapman). Dutfield's Yard, Berner Street, Whitechapel (Stride). Mitre Square, City of London (Eddowes). 13 Miller's Court, Dorset Street, Spitalfields (Kelly).
Dates: August 31st, 1888 (Nichols). September 8th, 1888 (Chapman). September 30th, 1888 (Stride and Eddowes). November 9th, 1888 (Kelly).
Means: Cutting of the throat, followed by post-mortem selective mutilation, with uterine bias, and evisceration.
Motive: Sexual gratification achieved by mutilation.
Crimewatch: Peripatetic sexual psychopath. Has been suggested that he first pointed his toe to England from Russia or Poland. Certainly beyond the Pale behaviour. Definitely no connection with the British royal family. Most unlikely to be any of the well-known personages bruited as the innominate one. Nor a cricketing barrister. Victims all prostitutes. Abdomens routinely ripped open. Dubiously alleged to have written taunting notes to the police. Vanished after fifth and final – indoor orgy – murder. Despite all and many subsequent rumours, no real clue to the Ripper's true identity has ever been discovered.

Prime sources: *The Identity of Jack the Ripper,* Donald McCormick, Jarrolds, London, 1959.

Jack the Ripper in Fact and Fiction, Robin Odell, Harrap, London, 1965.

Autumn of Terror, Tom A. Cullen, Bodley Head, London, 1965.

The Complete Jack the Ripper, Donald Rumbelow, W. H. Allen, London, 1975.

A Casebook on Jack the Ripper, Richard Whittington – Egan, Wildy & Sons, London, 1975.

The Crimes, Detection and Death of Jack the Ripper, Martin Fido, Weidenfeld & Nicolson, London, 1987.

Jack the Ripper: The Bloody Truth, Melvin Harris, Columbus Books, London, 1987.

The Ripper Legacy, Martin Howells & Keith Skinner, Sidgwick & Jackson, London, 1987.

Jack the Ripper: The Uncensored Facts, Paul Begg, Robson Books, London, 1988.

The Jack the Ripper A to Z, Paul Begg, Martin Fido and Keith Skinner, Headline, London, 1991.

Jack the Stripper

Irene Lockwood

The Hammersmith Nudes Murders

Serial killer

Murderer: Jack the Stripper. Unidentified.

Victims: Hannah Tailford (30). Irene Lockwood (26). Helen Catherine Barthelemy (22). Mary Fleming (30). Margaret McGowan (21). Bridget (Bridie) Esther O'Hara (28). Possibly – Gwynneth Rees (22).

Loci: In the river Thames – bumping up against the pontoon pier beside the London Corinthian Club (of oarsmen), Hammersmith Reach, West London (Tailford). Floating among weeds and a tangle of bankside branches in the Thames at Duke's Meadow, a large area of riverside grassland at Chiswick, West London (Lockwood). In an alleyway ten yards off Swyncombe Avenue, Brentford, West London (Barthelemy). On the parking space in front of the garage of a house in Berrymede Road, Chiswick (Fleming). Under a pile of rubble in a car park in Hornton Street, 100 yards from Kensington High Street (McGowan). Sprawled on a bed of bracken behind a store-shed off Westfield Road, Acton, West London (O'Hara). In an ash-tip near Chiswick Bridge (Rees).

Dates: Bodies discovered: February 2nd, 1964 (Tailford). April 8th, 1964 (Lockwood). April 24th, 1964 (Barthelemy). July 14th, 1964 (Fleming). November 25th, 1964 (McGowan). February 16th, 1965 (O'Hara). November 8th, 1963 (Rees).

Means: Exact cause of death of Tailford unestablished, but head injuries indicate possible knocking about. Exact cause of Lockwood's death not known, but marks on back of head. Strangulation (Barthelemy, McGowan, O'Hara). Cause of death of

Rees unascertainable.

Motive: Sexual alleviation. Ex-Detective Assistant Commissioner John du Rose, in charge of the investigation, believed the killer to be a man in his forties who originally formed no intent to kill, but was subject to orgasmic frenzy in which the women died. A curious feature was the extraction of teeth post-mortem. Three of Barthelemy's front teeth were missing and one of McGowan's.

Crimewatch: As Jack the Ripper flitted through the pea-soupers and yellow gaslight of the East End of the 1880s, so did Jack the Stripper move shadowlike amid the rubbish tips, across industrial estates and down black towpaths of the West London riverside of the 1960s. All his victims were prostitutes working the North Kensington, Bayswater and Soho areas. All were small in size, between 4ft. and 5ft. 3in., three at least bore tattooes, all were found naked. Whether Rees was his seventh victim is questionable. The other six were picked up, driven by car or van to the killing spot and attacked from behind. After death the body was stripped, stored somewhere where sprayed paint microscopically contaminated it, and, later, wrapped in a tarpaulin and dumped. Vital clues: tiny multicoloured specks of paints, found on Barthelemy, Fleming and McGowan, and the fact that O'Hara's corpse was partly mummified, which indicated storage near a heat-source. Samples of paint flakes found beneath a covered transformer (heat source) behind a building on the Heron Estate, Acton, facing a paint-spray shop. That victims vanished between 11 p.m. and 1 a.m. and were dumped between 5 a.m. and 6 a.m., suggested a nightworker. Nightwatchman? Policeman? Security guard? It has been said – but with absolutely nothing to substantiate it – that a man who committed suicide in South London in March 1965 was Jack the Stripper.

Prime sources: *Murder Was My Business,* John du Rose, W. H. Allen, London, 1971.
Found Naked and Dead, Brian McConnell, New English Library, London, 1974.

Dr. Mario Jascalevich

'Dr. X'

Accused: Dr. Mario Jascalevich.
Victims: Carl Rohrbeck (73). Nancy Savino (4).
Margaret Henderson (26). Frank Biggs (59). Emma
Arzt (70).
Locus: Riverdell Hospital, Bergenfield, New Jersey.
Dates: December 13th, 1965 (Rohrbeck). March
20th, 1966 (Savino). April 23rd, 1966 (Henderson).
August 28th, 1966 (Biggs). September 23rd, 1966
(Arzt).
Means: It was alleged that Jascalevich administered
a lethal dose of curare by route of intravenous drip.
Motive: 'He wanted to have the power of life and
death in this hospital as chief of surgery. He wanted
to play God.' – words of State attorney, Sybil Moses.
Professional jealousy.
Crimewatch: The defence was that Dr. Jascalevich
was the victim of a conspiracy – 'political profit.
Pulitzer-book profit, prosecutor-judge profit.' The
doctor was seen near the victims of unexpected
death, but 'There is no proof that this man ever put
anything into anybody.' Curare was found in his
locker, but he claimed that he used it for vivisection
on dogs. Although there was suspicion and enquiry
in 1966, Jascalevich was not tried until 1976, when,
aged 51, he was acquitted on all charges. The
scientific proof of curare found in exhumed bodies
ten years interred had been hotly debated.
Jascalevich is said to have removed to Argentina.
Prime sources: *Final Treatment,* Matthew L. Lifflander, W.
W. Norton, New York, 1979.
Somebody is Lying: The Story of Dr. X, Myron Farber,
Doubleday, New York, 1982.

Patrick Wayne Kearney

The Trash Bag Murders

Serial killer

Murderer: Patrick Wayne Kearney.
Victims: Probable total of 32 male homosexual victims. Indicted for the killing of Albert Riviera (21). Arturo Marquez (24). John Le May (17).
Loci: Dumped along the highway, right from south Los Angeles, following the California coastline, to Newport Beach, down towards the Mexico border. Dismembered portions discovered in ditches by the roadside and on freeway shoulders, obviously thrown from a car. A plastic-wrapped head turned up on the conveyor belt at a recycling plant. A left leg was found on a junk heap outside a Sunset Beach saloon. *Dates:*   1972-77. The first of the bodies was discovered on Christmas Day 1972.
Means: Shooting in the head with small-calibre gun. All the victims were nude. Several were dismembered after being shot.
Motive: Almost all the victims were young male drifters haunting the homosexual cruising areas and hangouts around Hollywood and LA. Kearney specifically refused to articulate any motive for his gay slaughtering spree.
Crimewatch: Bearded, bespectacled, 38-year-old (born 1940), avowed homosexual, Kearney had worked as an electronics engineer for the LA aerospace firm, Hughes Aircraft Co. For 15 years he had been room-mates with David D. Hill (34), his best friend. Latterly, they lived at Redondo Beach. In their home there investigators turned up a hacksaw stained with what proved to be Le May's blood. They found, too, hair and carpet fibres which matched those adhering to tape on victims' bodies. Kearney

and Hill, who had fled to Mexico, walked in on the authorities on July 1st, 1977, pointed to a wanted poster with their pictures on it, and announced, 'We're them.' They had listened to the advice of relatives to turn themselves in. On July 13th, 1977, Kearney was indicted on three counts of murder. Charges against Hill were not pressed for lack of evidence. After pleading guilty to 21 killings in exchange for the promise that he would not receive the death penalty, Kearney proceeded to provide details of a further 11 homosexual murders. In 1978, he was sentenced to life.

Prime source: Contemporary newspapers.

Edmund Emil Kemper

The Co-ed Killer

Serial killer

Murderer: Edmund Emil Kemper.
Victims: (At age of 15). His grandparents, Maude and Edmund Kemper. (At age of 23). Six hitch-hiking girl students: Mary Ann Pesce (18). Anita Luchessa (18). Aiko Koo (15). Cindy Schall (18). Rosalind Thorpe (23). Alice Lui (21). His own mother, remarried and now Clarnell Strandberg, and her friend, Mrs. Sara (Sally) Taylor Hallett.
Loci: The Kemper farm at North Fork, near Tollhouse, Madera County, California (Grandparents). Side roads in Central California (Hitch-hikers). A duplex numbered 609A Ord Drive, Aptos, Santa Cruz, California (Mother and friend).
Dates.   1969-73
Means: Shooting, strangling, butchering. For mother – a blow with a claw-hammer.
Motive: A mixed psychopathology. Resentment of mother-figures. Sexual gratification (rape, necrophilia, cannibalism).
Crimewatch: Giant Kemper, 6ft 9in tall, 20 stone, with a high IQ of 136, was a child cat-killer and rejected by his parents. Mother used to lock him in the basement under a trap-door. Grandparents on a remote farm had a go at rearing him, but he repaid their strict kindness with a bullet in the head, and Grandma, writer of books for children, was also slashed to pieces with a knife. For this they sent him to Atascadero State Hospital, where he learnt all about rape. Released after five years, now aged 20 (born December 18th, 1948), rejected by the police as too tall, he found work as a flagman for the California Division of the Highways. Cruising the

freeways, he practised his technique in picking up student hitch-hikers. After rape his paramount pleasure was the dissection and decapitation of their bodies. He used a Polaroid as he was at his work. With a body in the boot of his car, he felt, he said, like a fisherman with a prize catch. He cooked and ate some bits. He decapitated his mother and her friend, too. Then – it was time – he gave himself up, pleaded insanity; but, on November 8th, 1973, was found guilty on all eight counts of first-degree murder and sentenced to life imprisonment.

Prime source: *The Co-ed Killer,* Margaret Cheney, Walker & Company, New York, 1976.

Constance Emily Kent

Murderer: Constance Emily Kent.

Victims: Francis Saville (Savile, Savill), Kent (3 years 10 months): half-brother.

Locus: Road Hill House, near Trowbridge, Wiltshire.

Date: June 29th, 1860.

Means: Throat cut with razor. Head practically severed from body. Stab wound in left side. Has been said that there was evidence of preliminary stifling.

Motive: To pay out stepmother (whose child he was) for taking the place of, and making disparaging remarks about, Constance's real mother and the children of the first marriage.

Crimewatch. Sixteen-year-old Constance was arrested for the murder but released by the Trowbridge magistrates. The child's nurse, Elizabeth Gough (22) was then accused. She, too, was discharged at the police court. The mystery seemed impenetrable until, five years later, Constance, who, under the benign influence of the Reverend Arthur Wagner, devout Puseyite, in whose Conventual Home of St. Mary, in Brighton, she had, in search of solitude and retreat, become a paying guest and most passionately embraced religion, came cathartically forward to confess her guilt. She who had sought revenge now sought redemption. Tried and found guilty at Salisbury Crown Court, spared death, her ordained purgatory was to spend the succeeding twenty years in prison. Released at the age of 41, calling herself now Ruth Emilie Kaye, she went to Australia. There she trained as a nurse and tended lepers and the tuberculous. Later she was appointed matron of an institution for problem girls, and finally became proprietress of a nurses' home in Maitland. Constance Kent died, aged 100, on April 10th, 1944, at Strathfield, New South Wales.

Prime sources: *The Great Crime of 1860,* J. W. Stapleton, E. Marlborough & Co., London, 1861.
The Road Murder: Being A Complete Report and Analysis, by A Barrister-At-Law, London n.d.
The Case of Constance Kent, John Rhode, Geoffrey Bles, London, 1928.
Saint – With Red Hands? Yseult Bridges, Jarrolds, London, 1954.
Cruelly Murdered, Bernard Taylor, Souvenir Press, London, 1979.

Peter Kürten

The Monster of Düsseldorf. The Düsseldorf Vampire

Serial killer

Murderer: Peter Kürten.

Victims: The full tally of his victims is unknown. He was charged with nine murders. Those of Christine Klein (10); Rosa Ohliger (8); Rudolf Scheer (45); Maria Hahn; Gertrud Hamacher (5); Luise Lenzen (14); Ida Reuter; Elisabeth Dörrier; Gertrud Albermann (5). He was also charged with seven attempted murders: Frau Kühn; Anna Goldhausen; Frau Mantel; Gustav Kornblum; Gertrud Schulte; Frau Meurer; Frau Wanders.

Loci: An inn on the Wolfsstrasse, Köln-Mülheim (Klein). Building site, Kettwiger-Strasse, in the Flingern district of western Düsseldorf (Ohliger). In the Hellweg, in the Flingern district of Düsseldorf (Scheer). A meadow close to the Morp-Papendell highway (Hahn). At Flehe, on the market garden allotments (Hamacher and Lenzen). Meadows beside the Rhine, near Düsseldorf (Reuter). On the banks of the Düssel near Grafenberg (Dörrier). The vicinity of the Haniel house near the Lenaustrasse, Düsseldorf (Albermann).

Dates: Summer, 1913 (Klein). February 8th, 1929 (Ohliger). February 12th, 1929 (Scheer). August 11th, 1929 (Hahn). August 24th, 1929 (Hamacher and Lenzen). September 29th, 1929 (Reuter). October 11th, 1929 (Dörrier). November 27th, 1929 (Albermann).

Means: Strangling, stabbing, throat-cutting, and bludgeoning.

Motive: Sadistic sexual gratification – especially satisfied by the sight of spurting blood.

Crimewatch: Born in Cologne-Mülheim, third of thirteen children of a brutal, alcoholic, incestuous father, Kürten was unquestionably the victim of a vicious background – bad home and poor heredity. Seduced, around age nine, to cruelty by a sadistic dog-catcher, he grew powerfully bonded to a sexuality fused with blood and suffering. He killed men, women, children, animals – anything he found – was an arsonist and a petty thief, and served many prison sentences. When he did work, it was as a sand moulder in a factory, where he was a very active trade unionist. Arrested in May 1930, he was tried in April 1931. During that waiting year his psychopathology was studied in great detail by psychiatrist Professor Karl Berg. Guillotined, aged 48, at Klingelputz prison, on July 2nd, 1932, after a hearty meal of Wiener-Schnitzel and white wine (second helpings) he went to his death proclaiming that the pleasure to end all pleasures would be to hear the sound of his own blood gushing from the stump of his neck.

Prime sources: *The Monster of Düsseldorf,* Margaret Seaton Wagner, Faber and Faber, London, 1932.
Peter Kürten, George Godwin, The Acorn Press, London, 1938.
The Sadist, Karl Berg, William Heinemann, London, 1945.

Leonard Lake

Serial killers

Charles Chitag Ng

Murderers: Leonard Lake aka Charles Gunnar, Paul Cosner, Scott Stapley. Charles Chitag Ng (pronounced Ing).

Victims: Made away with an estimated 25 men, women and children. Many of the decomposed remains still unidentified. Various friends, neighbours and chance acquaintances were murdered. Some victims had responded to advertisements offering video equipment for sale. Others, like Paul Cosner, came to sell a car to Lake. Known named victims include Kathy Allen, Brenda O'Connor, her friend Scott Stapley and her 2-year-old son, Lonnie Bond, Jr., (scattered baby teeth found), and, very probably, Lake's disagreeable younger brother, Donald, Lake's best friend from his Vietnam years, Charles Gunnar, and Ng's prison friend, Michael Carrol, whose girlfriend was Kathy Allen.

Loci: A survivalist compound at the Mother Lode, Humboldt County, California (Gunnar, Donald Lake). Two-room cabin off Blue Mountain Road, Wisleyville, Calaveras County, California. (Allen,

O'Connor, Bond and many others).

Dates: *c.* 1981-85.

Means: Not known (save in the cases of 'snuff' video victims) but assuredly following prolonged torture.

Motive: Complicated. Basically sexual, of course, but linked with a belief – perhaps genuine, perhaps adapted and adopted – that an inevitable nuclear holocaust impended.

Crimewatch: Lake – born July 20th, 1946, in San Francisco – balding, black-bearded, powerful-looking, former Marine and Vietnam veteran, was into war-games. Through this mutual interest met, in 1981, Ng (24), ex-Marine, ex-convict, fugitive. Lake had developed, too, an interest in survivalism. The stockpiling of food supplies, weapons and women sex slaves, through whom he would repopulate the post-holocaust world, went well with his obsessional personality, expressed in hypergraphia, compulsively minute genetic experimentation with rats and mice in his boyhood, the indulgence in continual hand-washing rituals and the absolute insistence that his victims should take a shower before the torture session began. On June 2nd, 1985, Ng was seen shoplifting at a San Francisco hardware store. He ran off, but Lake, arrested, committed suicide, swallowing a cyanide capsule. Police sent to search his house for other stolen goods found mutilated bodies, skeletal remains, torture implements and home-made 'snuff' videos, combining violent sex scenes with actual murders committed on camera. Ng, captured at Calgary, Alberta, Canada, in July 1985, after another shoplifting incident, is now serving a prison sentence there. All attempts at extradition have so far failed.

Prime source: Contemporary newspapers.

John Watson Laurie

The Arran Murder

Murderer: John Watson Laurie.
Victim: Edwin Robert Rose (32).
Locus: Goatfell, Isle of Arran, Scotland.
Date: July 15th, 1889.
Means: Probably battering with a stone.
Motive: Robbery, premeditated? Insane sudden impulse? Quarrel? Homosexual undertones?
Crimewatch: Two men went to climb, went to climb a mountain. One came down, The other stayed up hidden in a tomb of stones. Holiday acquaintances, Laurie (26), a skilled artisan, and Rose, a dandiacal clerk from Upper Tooting, were lodging together on the island. On July 15th, they began the ascent of Goatfell. Three hours later, a shepherd saw Laurie coming down alone. He left the island. Rose was missed on July 18th. On August 4th, a search-party of 200 tackled the misty mountain. A fisherman found Rose's robbed body hidden under stones plugged with heather. The face, left side of head, and left shoulder-blade were frightfully smashed. Run to earth in a wood near Glasgow, Laurie said, "I robbed the man, but I did not murder him." At the trial in Edinburgh on November 8th, 1889, the defence was that Rose had fallen to his death. Laurie was convicted by a majority of one, seven voting for Not Proven, but the death sentence was commuted to life after a petition claiming insanity. He died in Perth Criminal Asylum on October 4th, 1930.

Prime source: *Notable British Trial,* edited by William Roughead, William Hodge, Edinburgh, 1932.

Ronald Vivian Light

The Green Bicycle Case

Accused: Ronald Vivian Light.
Victim: Annie Bella Wright (21).
Locus: Gartree Road, also known as Via Devana,
near Little Stretton, Leicestershire.
Date: July 5th, 1919.
Means: Shooting in head.
Motive: Unknown.
Crimewatch: Ronald Light, born in October, 1885,
was recovering from shell-shock. When arrested, he
was a master at a school at Cheltenham. Giving
evidence on his own behalf, he admitted bicycling
with Bella Wright, whom he had not known
previously. He said that they had parted at a junction
near the spot where her dead body was found, a
spent bullet beside it. He admitted throwing his
green bicycle into a canal, because he was frightened.
The jury believed him. A dead rook or crow was
found nearby, and some there were who thought that
the shooting was an accident, perhaps a ricochet.

Prime sources: *The Green Bicycle Case,* H. R. Wakefield, Philip
Allan, London, 1930.
The Green Bicycle Mystery, A. W. P. Mackintosh, Published in
aid of the Bella Wright Memorial Fund, n.d.

Bobby Joe Long

Serial killer

Murderer: Bobby Joe Long.
Victims: The identities of all his 8 victims are not known. Generally accepted as his first victim was Ngeon Thi Long (19), a go-go dancer in the strip bars along North Nebraska Avenue, Tampa, Florida. Other named victims were Michelle Denise Simms (22), Virginia Johnson (18) and Kim Swann. Long was also the Classified Ad Rapist, operating in Fort Lauderdale and Ocala, Florida, raping and robbing housewives who innocently placed 'for sale' advertisements in the local newspapers. At that time he displayed no homicidal violence, but is reputed to have committed more than 50 rapes in Florida between 1980 and 1983.
Loci: A field outside Tampa (Ngeon Thi Long). Other bodies left along the side of the road in rural areas around Tampa.
Dates: May 1983 – November 1983. Body discovered May 13th, 1983 (Ngeon Thi Long). Body discovered May 27th, 1983 (Simms).
Means: Bound, strangled, sometimes stabbed to death.
Motive: To satisfy raging hypersexuality. During the latter part of his marriage was requiring intercourse two or three times a day, in addition to masturbation at least five or more times per day. Also, an element of revenge against womankind, as typified by his forceful mother and dictatorial ex-wife.
Crimewatch: Born in Kenova, West Virginia, October 14th, 1953. Presents a curious psychiatric history. At age 11, developed female breasts – a familial, congenital, endocrinal dysfunction

consequence – and became fearful of being transformed into a women. Surgically corrected, but continued to experience lunar premenstrual cycle. In 1973 married Cindy Jean Guthrie, whom he had been dating since he was 13. Two children. Divorced 1978. In 1973 Long, then serving in the Army, where he hoped to become a qualified electrician, sustained massive head injuries in a motorcycle accident. Said to have undergone personality change to hypersexuality and hair-trigger violence. Arrested November 16th 1984, after allowing a 17-year-old girl whom he had kidnapped and raped to go free to identify him, Long said that he was tired of killing and wanted to be caught. At his trial he pleaded guilty to seven murders and received six life sentences. For the murder of Virginia Johnson he was sentenced to death. When it was learned that Long had been interrogated by the police after he had requested a lawyer, the Florida Supreme Court ordered a new trial. At his second trial – in 1989 – the jury recommended the death penalty. He is currently on Death Row at Starke, Florida.

Prime source: Contemporary newspapers.

Henry Lee Lucas

Serial killer

Murderer: Henry Lee Lucas.

Victims: Has claimed between 360 and 600 killings. Subsequently retracted, saying that he had told tall tales because he enjoyed the notoriety and wanted to embarrass the police. Stated that he had committed only one murder – that of his mother. But convicted of three murders in Texas.

Loci: Based on original claims, wide-splaying blood trail striking across Arkansas, California, Florida, Georgia, Indiana, Illinois, Louisiana, Michigan, New Mexico, Ohio, Texas, Virginia, Washington and Wisconsin. Also a brief foray into Canada.

Dates: Mainly between 1975 and 1983.

Means: Stabbing, strangling, stomping, suffocating, hanging, bludgeoning and shooting. Liked to mutilate and dismember victims alive, and to fillet them like fish after old American Indian torture fashion.

Motive: Chiefly sexual gratification and spree-killing blood-lust, but with an infrastructure of pure hatred (especially in the case of his mother).

Crimewatch: Born August 23rd, 1936, in Virginia hill country. Son of unnamed client of his half-American Indian, half-Irish prostitute mother. Classic deprived childhood. Privation, severe physical and sexual abuse by mother and brutal live-in boyfriend. Dressed as a girl up to age 5. In and out of prison for theft from age 14. Sentenced to 40 years in 1960 for murdering his mother. Paroled in 1970, he warned 'If you release me now, I will kill again.' They did. And he did. Again . . . and again . . . and again . . . . In Jacksonville Prison for attempted abduction, 1970-

1975. Released and teamed up with homosexual, cannibalistic Ottis Elwood Toole (28). While living in a trailer on the camp ground of Pentecostal preacher Stanley Shane's community, House of Prayer For All People, at Stoneburg, Texas, Lucas stabbed to death Becky Powell, his 15-year-old common law wife, with whom he had been living since she was nine, and knifed Katherine Rich (80). He was arrested on June 11th, 1983. Most unusually for a serial killer, Lucas purports to have undergone a death-cell religious conversion. A committed Christian, he awaits events on Death Row, Huntsville, Texas.

Prime sources: *Hand of Death,* Max Call, Prescott Press, Lafayette, Louisiana, 1985.
The Confession of Henry Lee Lucas, Mike Cox, Pocket Star Books, New York, 1991.

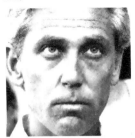

Dr. Jeffrey R. MacDonald

Murderer: Dr. Jeffrey R. MacDonald.
Victims: Colette S. MacDonald (26): wife. Kimberley K. MacDonald (5): daughter. Kristen J. MacDonald (2): daughter.
Locus: 544 Castle Drive, Corregidor Courts, Fort Bragg, Fayetteville, North Carolina.
Date: February 17th, 1970.
Means: Stabbing 16 times with a knife and 21 times with an icepick. Also six blows with a club (Colette). Three blows with a club and 8 to 10 stabbings with a knife (Kimberley). Thirty-three stabbings with a knife and an ice pick (Kristen).
Motive: Uncontrollable rage, without premeditation. A matrimonial quarrel that flared into homicide and was then compounded to mimic a Manson-like massacre.
Crimewatch: Dr. MacDonald, an achiever, aged 26, was a serving medical officer with the Green Berets. Joe McGinniss, in *Fatal Vision,* makes much of the doctor's ingestion of amphetamines before the tragedy, but MacDonald always claimed that four intruders did the killings; they said "Kill the pigs", and "Acid is groovy." MacDonald himself was found with minor injuries and a partially collapsed lung. A drug-addicted girl, Helena Stoeckley, confessed and retracted. More than nine years after the killings, MacDonald was finally tried at Raleigh, North Carolina, and found guilty of second-degree murder of Colette and Kimberley, and of first-degree murder of Kristen. August 29th, 1979, given three life sentences.
Prime source: *Fatal Vision,* Joe McGinniss, Putnam, New York, 1983.

Patrick David Mackay

Mass murderer

Murderer: Patrick David Mackay.
Victims: Isabella Griffiths (84): widow who had befriended MacKay. Adele Price (89): widow, a stranger, who offered him a glass of water. Father Anthony Crean (64): priest, a friend, from whom MacKay had stolen money.
Loci: 19 Cheyne Walk, Chelsea, London (Griffiths). Lowndes Square, London (Price). The Malt House, St. Catherine's Convent, Shorne, Kent (Crean).
Dates: February 14th, 1974 (Griffiths). March 10th, 1975 (Price). March 21st, 1975 (Crean).
Means: Manual strangulation and stabbing with a 12-inch kitchen knife (Griffiths). Manual strangulation (Price). Axe and knife (Crean).
Motive: No rational motive; psychopathic rage – frenzy – triggered by minor rejections, taunts, alcohol, drugs, despair and loneliness.
Crimewatch: Bad case of a gross personality disorder, diagnosed early, in and out of institutions, dangerously out of control, and a heavy drinker. IQ 92. His father, violent, and an alcoholic. As a boy MacKay tortured animals, and was preoccupied with Nazism, calling himself 'Franklin Bollvolt the First.' At the Old Bailey on November 21st, 1975, he came easily under the umbrella of 'Diminished Responsibility'. Sentenced, aged 23, to life for manslaughter of three. Two killings left on file and 24 muggings.

Prime source: *Psychopath,* Tim Clark and John Penycate, Routledge and Kegan Paul, London, 1976.

Jessie M'Lachlan

The Sandyford Mystery

Murderer: Jessie M'Lachlan.
Victim: Jessie M'Pherson (c. 38).
Locus: The basement of 17 Sandyford Place,
Glasgow.
Date: July 4th – 5th, 1862.
Means: Ferocious attack with a butcher's cleaver.
Motive: According to the prosecution of M'Lachlan,
financial gain. But all very dubious. See below.
Crimewatch: While 78-year-old James Fleming's
widowed son and grandson went away to Dunoon for
the weekend, he was left with the young maid, Jessie
M'Pherson. On the family's return, Jessie was found
near-naked and dead in her bedroom. On the
floorboards were imprints in blood of a naked foot.
There were signs of a severe struggle in the kitchen.
Some silver spoons were missing. Also garments from
the dead servant's box. M'Pherson's friend, Jessie
M'Lachlan, (29) who had called on her that fatal
Friday night, was arrested. She had pawned the
missing spoons. She had had possession of
M'Pherson's clothes. Her foot matched the bloody
imprint. Tried at Glasgow, she entered the special
defence that the chief Crown witness, Auld Fleming,
who had an unsavoury reputation with women and
who had originally been arrested, had committed the
crime. He had, she said, been forcing his attentions
on M'Pherson. There was a quarrel and he killed her.
M'Lachlan had been there and seen it all. She was not
believed. Found guilty and sentenced to death, she
was reprieved. Her 15 years in Perth prison were most
likely a miscarriage of justice. Released, she went to
America, dying in 1899 at Port Huron, Michigan.

Prime sources: *The Sandyford Murder Case,* J. H. Hastings, Glasgow, 1862.

The Sandyford Murder: A Plea For Mrs. M'Lachlan, A Clergyman of the Church of Scotland, Thomas Murray & Son, Glasgow, 1862.

Notable Scottish Trial, edited by William Roughead, William Hodge, Edinburgh, 1911.

Heaven Knows Who, Christianna Brand, Michael Joseph, London, 1960.

Charles Milles Manson

Mass murderer

Murderer: Charles Milles Manson.
Victims: Gary Hinman (34). Sharon Marie Tate or Polanski (26). Abigail Anne Folger (25). Wojciech 'Voyteck' Frykowski (32). Jay Sebring (35). Steven Parent (18). Rosemary LaBianca (38). Leno LaBianca (44). Donald Jerome 'Shorty' Shea (36).
Loci: 964 Old Topanga Road, Malibu (Hinman). 10050 Cielo Drive, Los Angeles. (Sharon Tate killings). 3301 Waverley Drive, Los Angeles (LaBianca Killings). Spahn Movie Ranch, 12000 Santa Susanna Pass Road, Los Angeles (Shea).
Dates: July 27th, 1969 (Hinman). August 9th, 1969 (Tate, Folger, Frykowski, Sebring, Parent) August 10th, 1969 (the LaBiancas). August 25th or 26th, 1969 (Shea).
Means: Multiple stabbings and shootings, sometimes in concert.
Motive: Manson's followers, particularly the besotted, drop-out girls, sodden with drugs, acted at his behest and in fear of him and their peers. Manson pushed them as far as he could. This was mainly killing for pleasure. Otherwise, young Parent was in the way, and cowboy Shorty Shea knew too much. Although partly motivated by blood-lust in the cases of the transported executants, these were not serial murders, as the inciter, at a remove, had his own psychopathological, sociologic reasons, which had little to do with either sex or enjoyment.
Crimewatch: Manson incited to murder. Apart from his 9 murder convictions, there were other killings by the Manson Family – the total may be about 35. From his free-range hippy commune in the desert, with its

free-for-all of sex and drugs, and rattlesnakes, he sent forth his murder squads to 'off' representative pockets of the rich and privileged. His converts enjoyed the blood-release. An elaborate delusional system based on 'Helter-Skelter', from an interpretation of the Beatles' song, with the murders acting as a warning against a black uprising, was imputed to Manson, who was, indeed, diagnosed in prison as paranoid and schizophrenic, but, a shrewd old gaolbird (born November 12th, 1934), he later repudiated his apocalyptic ideas and his Satanic image. He serves life in San Quentin.

Prime sources: *Witness to Evil,* George Bishop, Nash Publishing, Los Angeles, 1971.
The Family, Ed Sanders, Rupert Hart-Davis, London, 1971.
The Manson Murders, Victor Bugliosi & Curt Gentry, Bodley Head, London, 1974.
Without Conscience, Charles Manson & Nuel Emmons, Grafton Books, London, 1987.

Peter Thomas Anthony Manuel

Serial killer

Murderer: Peter Thomas Anthony Manuel.
Victims: Anne Knielands (17). Marion Watt (45).
Vivienne Watt (16): daughter. Margaret Brown (41):
sister. Isabelle Cooke (17). Peter Smart (45). Doris
Smart: wife. Michael Smart (11): son.
Loci: All the killings were restricted to a 24-square-
mile expanse of Lowland Scotland situated to the
east and south-east of Glasgow. Capelrig Copse, East
Kilbride Golf Course (Knielands). 5 Fennsbank
Avenue, High Burnside (The Watts). Ploughed field,
Burntbroom Farm, Mount Vernon (Cooke). 38
Sheepburn Road, Uddingston (The Smarts).
Dates: January 2nd, 1956 (Knielands). September
16th, 1957 (The Watts). December 28th, 1957
(Cooke). January 1st, 1958 (The Smarts).
Means: Battering with iron bar (Knielands).
Shooting with Webley .38 revolver (The Watts).
Shooting with Beretta pistol (The Smarts). Strangling
with brassière (Cooke).
Motive: Manuel killed for pleasure and sexual
gratification. He was a known sex offender with a
history of indecent assaults and rapes.
Crimewatch: Born on March 15th, 1927, in
Manhattan, his parents having emigrated to America
in search of work. He returned with them to Britain
in 1932, and, after a youth dedicated to petty theft
and burglarious enterprise and, in consequence,
spent largely in approved schools and Borstals, he
was, unmarried, living in 1956 with his father and
mother at 32 Fourth Street, Birkenshaw, in the
centre of the killing territory. A classic psychopath,
boastful, a liar and a loner who loved the dark, he

was also clever and competitive. He liked to 'take on' and 'best' the police. It came to their ears that Manuel was spending recklessly. They searched his home and found burglary loot there. Arrested on January 14th, 1958, and charged with the Smart murders. He did all he could to impeach the Crown witness, William Watt, sole surviving member of the murdered family. Tried at Glasgow High Court, May 1958, before Lord Cameron, Manuel elected to conduct his own defence – which he did surprisingly adroitly. He was found guilty of 7 of the 8 charges. No corroborative evidence – as required in Scots law – was forthcoming in regard to the killing of Anne Knielands. Hanged at Barlinnie prison, July 11th, 1958. Before his execution he confessed to the murders and those of Helen Carlin, prostitute, strangled in Pimlico, September 1954; Anne Steele (55) spinster, battered to death, Glasgow, January 11th, 1956; Ellen Petrie, stabbed, Glasgow, 15th June 1956. He is thought to have murdered also Sydney Dunn (37), c. December 6th/7th, 1957, a taxidriver, found shot and with gashed throat on the moors near Edmondbyers, County Durham.

Prime sources. *The Trial of Peter Manuel,* John Gray Wilson Secker & Warburg, London, 1959.
The Hunting Down of Peter Manuel, John Bingham, Macmillan, London, 1973.

Florence Elizabeth Maybrick

Murderer: Florence Elizabeth Maybrick.
Victim: James Maybrick: husband (50).
Locus: Battlecrease House, 7 Riversdale Road,
Aigburth, Liverpool.
Date: May 11th, 1889.
Means: Arsenic.
Motive: To be rid of a choleric, faithless husband.
Crimewatch: Highly contentious Victorian cause
célèbre. Not even proved that habitual drug- and
nostrum-swallowing James Maybrick did in fact die of
arsenical poisoning. His American wife, Florence –
born September 3rd, 1862, Mobile, Alabama –
mother of two, James and Gladys, was condemned as
much as anything for her discovered adultery with
Maybrick's fellow cotton broker, Alfred Brierley. That
James had a mistress and several illegitimate children
did not count. Undeniably, the Maybricks – he 50,
she 26 – had not a happy marriage. It came to blows,
he administering a black eye to her following a
quarrel over Brierley at the Grand National race
course on March 29th, 1889. Seen by a servant
soaking flypapers in water, Florence said it was to
obtain arsenic for a face lotion. Others put a more
sinister interpretation on it when Maybrick died.
Tried in St. George's Hall, Liverpool, she was
convicted, sentenced to hang and reprieved. After
serving 15 years she returned in 1904 to America,
surviving to a poverty-stricken, eccentric old age,
dying as Mrs. Chandler, the Cat Woman, in a
tumbledown shack near South Kent, Connecticut, on
October 23rd, 1941. A deceitful, untruthful, light-
fingered woman it is alleged, it later emerged that, in

the last week of April 1889, she had obtained from a Liverpool chemist, Richard Aspinall, of Leece Street, a quantity of 'Arsenic for Cats' without signing his Poisons Book.

Prime sources: *The Maybrick Case,* Alexander William MacDougall, Baillière, Tindall and Cox, London, 1891.
The Necessity For Criminal Appeal as Illustrated by the Maybrick Case, J. H. Levy, P. S. King and Son, London, 1899.
Notable English Trial, edited by H. B. Irving, William Hodge, Edinburgh, 1912.
This Friendless Lady, Nigel Morland, Frederick Muller, London, 1957.
Etched in Arsenic, Trevor L. Christie, Harrap, London, 1969.
The Poisoned Life of Mrs. Maybrick, Bernard Ryan with Sir Michael Havers, QC, MP, William Kimber, London, 1977.
My Fifteen Lost Years, Florence Elizabeth Maybrick, Funk & Wagnalls, New York, 1905.

John Donald Merrett

alias Ronald John Chesney

Murderer: John Donald Merrett alias Ronald John Chesney.

Victims: Mrs. Bertha Merrett (56): mother. Isobel Veronica Chesney (42): wife. Mrs. Mary Bonnar, Lady Menzies (68): mother-in-law.

Loci: 31 Buckingham Terrace, Edinburgh (Bertha Merrett). 22 Montpelier Road, Ealing, London (Isobel Veronica Chesney, Lady Menzies).

Dates: March 17th, 1926 (Mrs. Bertha Merrett). February 11th, 1954 (Vera Chesney, Lady Menzies/Bonnar).

Means: Shot with .25 Spanish automatic pistol (Mrs. Bertha Merrett). Drowned in bath (Vera Chesney), strangled with a stocking (Lady Menzies).

Motive: For his convenience.

Crimewatch: As there are two names for this man, so are there two views as to his persona. There is John Donald Merrett, the cheating son who robbed his mother, first of her money, then of her life. And there is Ronald John Chesney, the flamboyant, fun-loving, swashbuckling buccaneer, who drowned his wife and strangled his mother-in-law. Both Merrett and Chesney died when, having reached the end of his hawser, the huge, 22-stone, bearded giant shot himself with his Colt .45 in a wood outside Cologne on February 16th, 1954, mourned only by his faithful German mistress, Gerda Schaller. Born in New Zealand on August 17th, 1908. His parents drifted apart. Came with his Manchester-raised mother, who doted on Donald, to Britain in 1924. Highly intelligent; highly undisciplined. Sent first to Malvern College, then Edinburgh University. Got away with the murder of his mother. Imprisoned for forging her cheques. Became a naval officer, serving with courageous but reckless seamanship which earned him the nickname 'Crasher' Chesney. Bully, braggart, glutton, vast drinker, gambler, smuggler, hot-blooded lover, cold-blooded killer, Merrett was a monumental self-indulger, the complete psychopath, prepared to sacrifice anyone or anything at the altar of his own sacred desires.

Prime sources: *Notable British Trial,* edited by William Roughead, William Hodge, Edinburgh, 1929.
Portrait of a Bad Man, Tom Tullett, Evans Brothers, London, 1956.
Chesney: The Fabulous Murderer, Hugh McLeave, Pinnacle Books, London, n.d.

Louisa May Merrifield

Murderer: Louisa May Merrifield.
Victim: Sarah Ann Ricketts (79).
Locus: The Homestead, 339 Devonshire Road, North Shore, Blackpool.
Date: April 14th, 1953.
Means: Phosphorus (Rodine rat poison).
Motive: Gain.

Crimewatch. The Merrifields went in answer to an advertisement as live-in housekeepers to Mrs. Ricketts. During the honeymoon period all was sweetness and light. That was when, after a mere twelve days, Mrs. Ricketts made her fatal mistake. She confided that she was going to bequeath the bungalow to them. But the Merrifields rapidly became disenchanted with their "invalid lady". She began to display tantrums. She showed herself as awkward, impatient, disagreeable, and an alcoholic into the bargain. Louisa May, strict Baptist and a Wigan miner's daughter, married, aged 25, Joseph Ellison, and had four children, who were taken into care because of her drinking and negligence. Ellison died in 1949. Three months after his death she, then 42, married 78-year-old Richard Weston. Ten weeks later he was dead. In 1950, she married Merrifield (67). She felt they had landed on their feet at The Homestead – but couldn't wait to get their hands on their inheritance. Tried at Manchester, Mrs. Merrifield was hanged at Strangeways on September 18th, 1953. She was 46. The Attorney-General having entered a *nolle prosequi*, Alfred Merrifield was released. He died, aged 80, in 1962.

Prime source: Contemporary newspapers.

Herman Webster Mudgett alias H. H. Holmes

Mass murderer

Murderer: Herman Webster Mudgett aka H. H. Holmes.

Victims: Admitted to killing 27 people. Then retracted, claiming two deaths only – resultant upon illegal operations. Thought to have murdered 150-200, mainly women and children.

Loci: 701-703 Sixty-Third Street, Englewood, Chicago. (Scene of the mass murders.) Momence, Illinois (Minnie Williams). Leadville, Colorado (Baldwin Williams). 1316 Callowhill Street, Philadelphia (Benjamin Fuller Pitezel). Irvington, Indiana (Howard Pitezel). 16 Vincent Street, Toronto, Canada (Alice and Nellie Pitezel).

Dates: c 1891-94

Means: Varied: merciful chloroforming in sleep, savage butchery, gloating poison-gassing.

Motive: Financial profit – admixed with sexual advantages.

Crimewatch: Described as America's "arch-fiend of murder", Mudgett was essentially a swindler, but he was also a sadist who enjoyed murdering and torturing. An escalating career of fraud began with the theft of cadavers from his medical school – Ann Arbor, Michigan – and climaxed with his gothic 'murder factory', the Englewood 'hotel' nicknamed 'Holmes' Castle'. This was a maze of nearly 100 rooms, many hidden, with concealed staircases, trap-doors, torture chambers and a chute for bodies to slide down to a dissecting table, quick-lime pits, acid vats and a stove-cremator in the basement. For murdering his crooked associate, Benjamin F. Pitezel (whose three children he had also slaughtered)

Mudgett was hanged at Moyamensing Prison, Philadelphia, on May 7th, 1896, nine days before his 36th birthday.

Prime sources: *The Holmes-Pitezel Case,* Frank P. Geyer, Publishers' Union, Philadelphia, 1896.
The Trial of Herman W. Mudgett, George T. Bisel, Philadelphia, 1897.
The Girls in Nightmare House, Charles Boswell & Lewis Thompson, Gold Medal Books, Fawcett Publications, Greenwich, Connecticut, 1955.
The Torture Doctor, David Franke, Hawthorn Books, New York, 1975.

Herbert William Mullin

Mass murderer

Murderer: Herbert William Mullin.
Victims: Lawrence White (55). Mary Margaret Guilfoyle (24). Father Henri Tomei (65). James Ralph Gianera. Joan Gianera (21). Kathy Francis (29). Daemon Francis (4). David Hughes (9). David Allan Oliker (18). Robert Michael Spector (18). Brian Scott Card (19). Mark John Dreibelbis (15). Fred Abbie Perez (72).
Loci: Highway 9, Henry Cowell State Park, Canada del Rincon en el Rio section (White). Smith Grade junction with Empire Grade, mountain road north-east of Santa Cruz (Guilfoyle). St. Mary's Catholic Church, Los Gatos (Tomei). 520 Western Drive Santa Cruz (the Gianeras). Branciforte Drive, Santa Cruz (the Francis family). Henry Cowell State Park, Santa Cruz (Oliker, Spector, Card, Dreibelbis). Lighthouse Avenue, near Gharkey Street, Santa Cruz (Perez).
Dates: October 13th, 1972 (White). October 24th, 1972 (Guilfoyle). November 2nd, 1972 (Tomei). January 25th, 1973 (the Gianeras, the Francis family). February 6th, 1973 (Oliker, Spector, Card, Dreilbelbis). February 13th, 1973 (Perez).
Means: Beating to death with a baseball bat (White). Stabbing with hunting knife (Guilfoyle, Tomei). Shooting (the Gianeras, the Francis family, Oliker, Spector, Card, Dreibelbis, Perez).
Motive: An absolutely typical paranoid schizophrenic, he believed the voices which commanded him to offer human sacrifices to save California from impending earthquake disasters and also required him to kill for other, more arbitrary, reasons.

Crimewatch: Born April 18th, 1947. Oppressive Roman Catholic upbringing. Normal boyhood. Voted 'most likely to succeed' by his high school class. At 17 engaged to Loretta Ricketts. Close male friend, Dean Richardson, died in 1965 motor accident. Grief-stricken, Herb set up a shrine round Dean's photograph in his bedroom and told Loretta he was afraid he was homosexual. When he further announced himself a conscientious objector and went off to study religion in India, Loretta broke with him. By age 21 he was undergoing pronounced personality changes. He had smoked marijuana and taken LSD for years. He was hearing voices. They told him to shave his head and burn his genitals with a lighted cigarette. After hospital treatment, discharged early in 1970, he was back in hospital in Hawaii by the summer. Returned home – 1541 McLellan Road, Felton, California – in a disturbed state, he killed 13 times in Santa Cruz mountain country. Arrested – February 13th, 1973 – pleaded not guilty by reason of insanity. But the jury found him responsible. He is locked away until 2025. The case is held to demonstrate foolishness of state legislation which closed mental hospitals on grounds of economy and left psychotic time bombs like Mullin perilously at large.

Prime source: *The Die Song,* Donald T. Lunde and Jefferson Morgan, W. W. Norton, New York, 1980.

Donald Neilson

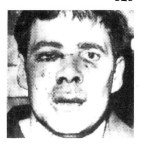

The Black Panther

Mass murderer

Murderer: Donald Neilson (born Donald Nappey).
Victims: Donald Lawson Skepper (54). Derek Astin
(43). Sidney James Grayland (56). Lesley Whittle
(17).
Loci: Sub-post office, Skipton Road, New Park,
Harrogate, Yorkshire (Skepper). Sub-post office,
Higher Baxenden, Accrington, Lancashire (Astin).
Sub-post office, High Street, Langley, West Midlands
(Grayland). Main shaft, Bathpool Park underground
drainage system, Kidsgrove, Staffordshire (Whittle).
Dates: February 15th, 1974 (Skepper). September
6th, 1974 (Astin). November 11th, 1974 (Grayland).
On a date unknown between January 13th and
March 7th, 1975 (Whittle).
Means: Sawn-off shotgun (Skepper). Sawn-off
shotgun and .22 pistol (Astin). .22 pistol (Grayland).
Vagal inhibition caused by suspension from a wire
attached to the neck (Whittle).
Motive: Financial gain – the pursuit of robbery (the
three shootings). Elimination of kidnap victim who
could identify him (Whittle).
Crimewatch: Did Lesley Whittle fall from the narrow
ledge in the shaft, or did Neilson push her off when
his kidnap plan went wrong? He said it was an
accident, that he saw her slip, and she was dead when
he left her. But then he said the post office shootings
were all accidents. The Defence well argued that if
the tethering wire had not snagged, the girl's feet
would have touched the ground. The wire was
padded with Elastoplast. Neilson claimed that he
always wore his panther hood and Lesley never saw
his face. Horribly, the post-mortem showed empty

stomach and intestines. Did he just abandon her?
Psychopath with paranoid and obsessional features,
who forced his wife and daughter to play war-games,
the Black Panther, aged 39, was caged for life.

Prime sources: *The Black Panther Story,* Steven Valentine,
New English Library, London, 1976.
The Capture of the Black Panther, Harry Hawkes, Harrap,
London, 1978.

Dennis Andrew Nilsen

Serial killer

Murderer: Dennis Andrew Nilsen.
Victims: Admitted slaying 15 or 16 young men.
Convicted of six murders. Kenneth James Ockendon
(23). Malcolm Barlow (23). Martyn Duffey (16). John
Peter Howlett. Billy Sutherland (27). Stephen
Sinclair (20). Archibald Graham Allen (28) was
identified too late to be included on the indictment.
Nilsen did not know the names of all his victims;
most, not all, were homosexual drifters. There were
also seven attempted murders.
Loci: Twelve or thirteen men were killed at 195
Melrose Avenue, Cricklewood, North London, and
three at his attic flat, 23 Cranley Gardens, Muswell
Hill, North London.
Dates: December 31st, 1978 – January 27th, 1983.
Means: Strangulation, sometimes in combination
with drowning.
Motive: Very murky psychopathology here. The
actual killing was important to Nilsen, but so, too,
was his contact with the freshly dead body: lying
beside and masturbating over it, and carrying out a
ritual of washing, drying and powdering. Any
necrophilic sexual connection was, said Nilsen, not
penetrative, but intercrural. The psychiatrists had a
field day.
Crimewatch: Lonely civil servant, frightening
fantasist, half in love with easeful death, Nilsen took
young men home from casual encounters in pubs.
Alcohol and music contributed to his mood. Disposal
of corpses was a problem. There was a useful garden
at Melrose Avenue. Bodies were stored under
floorboards, buried outside, stowed in suitcases in a

shed, and burnt on a bonfire. Cranley Gardens was more difficult, but not insurmountable. Bodies were dismembered in the bath, put out with garbage, dumped any old where, and flushed down the lavatory. The resultant blockage and the calling in of the man from Dyno-rod led to Nilsen's arrest. Police found, in a wardrobe, two plastic bags with mixed human remains, including two torsos, a boiled skull and another partially boiled head. Nilsen had used a large cooking-pot. In a tea-chest, another torso and skull. In a bag in the bathroom the lower half of Stephen Sinclair. At the Old Bailey, on November 4th, 1983, a jury rejected a plea of diminished responsibility and Nilsen was sentenced, aged 37, to life imprisonment.

Prime sources: *The Nilsen File,* Brian McConnell and Douglas Bence, Futura, Macdonald & Co., London, 1983. *House of Horrors,* John Lisners, Corgi Books, London, 1983. *Killing For Company,* Brian Masters, Jonathan Cape, London, 1985.

Christine Papin

Léa Papin

Murderers: Christine Papin and Léa Papin.
Victims: Madame Marie Lancelin. Geneviève
Lancelin (27): Daughter
Locus.   Le Mans, Sarthe Department, Western
France.
Date: February 2nd, 1933.
Means: Extreme violence. Gouging out of victims'
eyes, battering with pewter pot and hammer, attack
with knives
Motive: Never satisfactorily established. Speculation
postulates revenge, resentment, sheer bad temper, an
acte gratuit. But for some time an atmosphere had
been building in that house. Incidents, small in
themselves, had been piling up. Mme. Lancelin,
haughty, distant, speaking only to scold, was always
spying, counting the sugar lumps, running a white-
gloved finger along the furniture to check if the
dusting had been done properly. The slightest
damage was taken out of the Papin sisters' wages. The
heaviness became heavier; the stillness stiller, like the
air before a storm. What may have been the spark in
that *huis clos* was the blowing of the fuses by the iron.

The iron had gone wrong in January. It had been repaired – 5 francs out of the maids' wages on February 1st. The iron went wrong again on February 2nd, plunging the house in darkness. When Madame Lancelin and her daughter returned about 5 p.m. there was a scene. It escalated. Terrible bloodshed.

Crimewatch: When lawyer René Lancelin's wife and daughter did not arrive for dinner with him at a friend's, he hurried home to investigate. Finding his house dark and locked against him, he summoned the police. The first clue was a human eyeball caught in torchlight on the stair. On the first-floor landing lay the dead and mutilated bodies. The maids, cowering naked upstairs, admitted guilt. Christine (28) and Léa (21) were the products of a harsh background. They and their elder sister, Emilie, now a nun, had all been interfered with by a brutal drunkard father, from whom their mother separated in 1913. Brought up in convents and orphanages, the younger sisters went into service. In 1926 they came to work together at the Lancelins'. There were strong indications of a fierce lesbian relationship between them, but, specifically questioned by the judge, Christine, the dominant sister, flatly denied it. Tried in September 1933 at the Le Mans Palais de Justice, pleas of insanity failed. Both were found guilty. Léa was given 10 years' hard labour. Christine, sentenced to death, was reprieved. She died in Rennes asylum in 1937. Léa, released in 1942, went back to work as a chambermaid in good class French hotels.

Prime source: Contemporary newspapers.

Dr. Edward William Pritchard

Murderer: Dr. Edward William Pritchard.
Victims: Jane Taylor (70): mother-in-law. Mary Jane Pritchard (38): wife.
Locus: 131 Sauchiehall Street, Glasgow.
Dates: February 25th, 1865 (Taylor). March 18th, 1865 (Pritchard).
Means: Poisoning by a combination of antimony, aconite and opium.
Motive: Clearly to be rid of his wife. Mother-in-law had to go because she knew – or guessed – too much.
Crimewatch: Pritchard the poisoner was the very type specimen of the hypocrite, the weeper of crocodile tears. He shed them copiously over the open coffin of 'Mary Jane, my own beloved wife', whom he had been mercilessly slow-poisoning through endless weeks of agony. 'No torment surrounded her bedside,' he wrote in his diary, 'but, like a calm, peaceful lamb of God, passed Minnie away.' A liar as well as a lecher. Crafty, cruel, inordinately vain. But Pritchard is an enigma. Why did he elect to poison the wife and mother-in-law who worshipped him? Was it out of pure selfish boredom? Had he grown tired of his wife? Had his wandering eye fixed upon some possible future partner who might import wealth or social distinction? We can only speculate. There is not a speck of evidence. He was not a sadist. He would not kill for killing's sake. Only for his convenience. There is small doubt that, although he was never so charged, he was responsible for the death of Elizabeth M'Girn, the young servant-girl who perished in the fire he raised in his house at 11

Berkeley Terrace, Glasgow, on May 5th-6th, 1863. He also did his despicable best to cast suspicion of the poisonings of his wife and mother-in-law on 16-year-old Mary M'Leod, his maid-servant and his mistress. Mrs Taylor and Mrs Pritchard are buried in the Grange Cemetery in Edinburgh. A very gallant gentleman, the good Doctor was none the worse for a hanging – the last public execution in Glasgow, on the Green – on July 28th, 1865.

Prime sources: *A Complete Report of the Trial of Dr. E. W. Pritchard,* Reprinted by Special Permission, from the "Scotsman", Carefully Revised by An Eminent Lawyer, William Kay, Edinburgh, 1865.
Notable Scottish Trial, edited by William Roughead, William Hodge, Edinburgh, 1906.

Richard Leyva Ramirez

The Night Stalker

Serial killer

Murderer: Richard Leyva Ramirez.
Victims: Jennie Vincow (79). Dayle Okazaki (34).
Tsai-Lian Yu (30). Vincent Zazzara (64). Maxine
Zazzara (44): wife. Harold Wu aka William Doi (66).
Malvia Keller aka Mabel Bell (83). Patty Elaine
Higgins (32). Mary Louise Cannon (75). Joyce
Lucille Nelson (61). Maxson Kneiding (66). Lela
Kneiding (64): wife. Chitat Assawahem aka
Charnarong Khovanath (32). Ahmed Zia aka Elyas
Abowath (35). Peter Pan (66) and wife, Barbara (64).
Peter (66) and wife, Barbara (64) Pan.
Loci: Glassell Park, Eagle Rock, LA (Vincow).
Rosemead, LA (Okazaki). North Alhambra Drive,
Monterey Park, LA (Yu). Whittier, LA (Zazzara).
Monterey Park, LA (Wu, Nelson). Monrovia, LA
(Keller). Arcadia, LA (Higgins, Cannon). Stanley
Avenue, Glendale, LA (Kneiding). Sun Valley, LA
(Assawahem). Diamond Bar, San Gabriel Valley
(Zia). Lake Merced, San Francisco (Pan).
Dates: June 1984 – August 1985.
Means: Shooting (Okazaki, Yu, Wu, Kneiding,
Assawahem, Zia). Stabbing (Zazzara). Bludgeoning
(Keller). Throat-cutting (Vincow, Higgins, Cannon).
Beating to death (Nelson).
Motive: Sadistic sexual satisfaction expediently
linked with robbery.
Crimewatch: Light-fingered Hispanic sneak thief,
born in El Paso, Texas, February 28th, 1960.
Thumbnail-sketched as 'a confused, angry loner who
sought refuge in thievery, drugs, the dark side of
rock music – and, finally murder and rape.' Self-
proclaimed Satanist, living a street life of drugs and

junk food, was obsessed with 'Night Prowler', recorded by mock-Satanic 'heavy metal' group AC/DC. Unlike the majority of serial killers, who target drifters, prostitutes and alcoholics, he selected middle class rich, or at least well-heeled, victims. He would break into random houses by night to steal, would shoot or stab men as they slept and beat, rape, sexually abuse and, often, murder women, regardless of age. Would also sexually abuse, but not kill, children of both sexes. Used to draw occult signs, such as pentagrams, on the victim's body or the wall above it. The extreme savagery of his attacks led to a reign of terror in LA. He gouged out one victim's eyes and took them away with him. They were never found. Identified by a smudged fingerprint lifted from a stolen car and submitted to the just newly computerised fingerprint records system. Police plastered Ramirez's picture everywhere. Recognised in Tito's Liquor Store, 819 Towne Avenue, he was chased and captured by an angry mob of LA citizens on August 31st, 1985. Tried in 1989. Sentenced to die in the gas chamber, he is currently on Death Row in San Quentin.

Prime source; *Night Stalker*, Clifford L. Linedecker, St. Martin's Paperbacks, New York, 1991.

Dr. Buck Ruxton

Murderer: Dr. Buck Ruxton, originally Bukhtyar Rustomji Rantanji Hakim.
Victims: 'Mrs.' Isabella Ruxton (34) and Mary Jane Rogerson (20): her maid.
Locus: 2 Dalton Square, Lancaster, Lancashire.
Date: September 15th, 1935.
Means: Such was the fragmented state of the two bodies that certainty must be absent. Probably strangulation.
Motive: Gross morbid jealousy directed towards the wife, and elimination of the maid as a witness to the killing.
Crimewatch: Dr. Ruxton anatomised both bodies to avoid identification and to render them conveniently portable. He drove them by car to a bridge on the Edinburgh-Carlisle road, about two miles north of Moffat. Thence, at the place called the Devil's Beef Tub, he cast them down into the ravine along which runs a stream named Gardenholme Linn. On September 29th the remains were spotted. Weirdly, a 'Cyclops eye', probably from a lamb, was found amongst the *disjecta membra.* Ruxton, born in 1899, was hanged at Strangeways Prison, Manchester, on May 12th, 1936. The bath used by him in dismembering the bodies is now a horse-trough at Lancashire Constabulary Headquarters, Hutton, Preston.

Prime sources: *Notable British Trial,* edited by R. H. Blundell & G. Haswell Wilson, William Hodge, Edinburgh, 1937.
Medico-Legal Aspects of the Ruxton Case, John Glaister & James Couper Brash, E. & S. Livingstone, Edinburgh, 1937.
The Deadly Dr. Ruxton, T. F. Potter, Carnegie Press, Preston, Lancashire, 1984.

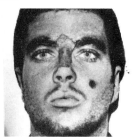

Charles Howard Schmid

Murderer: Charles Howard Schmid.
Victims: Norma Alleen Rowe (15). Gretchen Fritz (17). Wendy Fritz (13).
Loci: Killed and buried in the Arizona desert (Rowe). Killed at Schmid's cottage in Tucson. Bodies left out in the Arizona desert (the Fritz sisters).
Dates: May 31st, 1964 (Rowe). August 16th, 1965 (the Fritz sisters).
Means: Battering to death with a rock (Rowe). Strangling (the Fritz sisters).
Motive: Thrill killing admixed with jealousy in the case of Gretchen Fritz.
Crimewatch: Born July 8th, 1942. Pampered adopted son of Charles and Katharine Schmid, prosperous proprietors of the Tucson, Arizona, Hillcrest, Nursing Home. Young 'Smitty' had a problem. His height. 5ft 3in. At school he compensated by becoming a champion gymnast. Later, be became a tall-story-telling guru or Pied Piper for the bored teenagers of Tucson. At his small house opposite the nursing home, gift of his parents, he presided, Manson-like, over his drink- and drug-fixed followers and seduced the young girls. To create a macho image, he deep-tanned his face with pancake make-up, built up a huge black mole with putty on his left cheek, stuffed his cowboy boots with tin cans and rags to give him inches, and explained his resultant awkward walk as aftermath of a crippling fight with the Mafia. Bored with mere sex, he turned, aided and abetted by girlfriend Mary Rae French (19) and John Saunders (18), to murder. Their victim was Alleen Rowe. Smitty killed another

girlfriend, Gretchen Fritz, and her sister, Wendy, unaided, but his friend, Richard Bruns (19) helped bury them. Bruns' nerve broke. He told the police. Schmid is serving two terms of life. Saunders got life. French, 4-5 years.

Prime sources: *The Pied Piper of Tucson,* Don Moser and Jerry Cohen, New American Library, New York, 1967.
The Tucson Murders, John Gilmore, The Dial Press, New York, 1970.

Dr. Samuel Holmes Sheppard

Murderer: Dr. Samuel Holmes Sheppard.
Victim: Marilyn Reese Sheppard (31): wife.
Locus: 28924 Lake Road, Bay Village, Ohio.
Date: July 4th, 1954.
Means: Thirty-five blows to the head.
Motive: According to the Prosecution, a marital quarrel. Sheppard had not been faithful, and he admitted that Marilyn knew so.
Crimewatch: According to the Accused (surgeon, aged 30), the murderer was a bushy-haired intruder, who knocked him unconscious. Sheppard did, indeed, suffer a fractured cervical vertebra and concussion. Tried in Cleveland, Ohio, he was found guilty on December 21st, 1954, of murder in the second degree. Tragedy clung to the case. One Juror committed suicide; Dr. Sheppard's mother shot herself; eleven days later, his father died of gastric ulcer; Marilyn's father shot himself. Celebrated trial lawyer, F. Lee Bailey, took an interest. After re-trial, Sheppard was, on November 16th, 1966, acquitted. Released, he married Ariane Tebbenjohanns, but four-and-a-half years later she divorced him, claiming extreme cruelty. He took up professional wrestling for charity, and married the 19-year-old daughter of his wrestling manager. On April 6th, 1970, he died of liver failure.

Prime sources: *The Sheppard Murder Case,* Paul Holmes, Cassell, London, 1962.
Endure and Conquer, Dr. Sam Sheppard, The World Publishing Company, Cleveland, Ohio, 1966.
Dr. Sam: An American Tragedy, Jack Harrison Pollack, Henry Regnery Company, Chicago, 1972.

Oscar Slater

Accused: Oscar Slater or Oscar Leschziner.
Victim: Marion Gilchrist (82).
Locus: 15 Queen's Terrace, 49 West Princes Street, Glasgow.
Date: December 21st, 1908.
Means: Battered to death. No weapon found. Possibility suggested that the leg of a chair might have inflicted the injuries.
Motive: No clear motive ever advanced. One possibility punted was that of interrupted robbery.
Crimewatch: In the absence of the maid, Helen Lambie, between 7 and 7.15 p.m., someone succeeded in gaining entrance to the normally hyper-secured flat and felled the old lady. No forced entry. No robbery. Some ransacking. One small diamond crescent brooch said to be missing. Never found. Although Slater served 18½ years in prison for this murder before being grudgingly released on licence in 1927, the true culprit has never been identified. A Secret Inquiry held in 1914 merely confounded the confusion and brought another, totally blameless, man, Dr. Francis Charteris, under suspicion as bogus as that attaching to the Great Suspect, Slater. Strange 'evidence' provided by Glasgow detective, Lieutenant John Thomson Trench, backed up by Glasgow solicitor, David Cook, and later widely disseminated by Glasgow crusading journalist, William Park, drew Sir Arthur Conan Doyle and Edinburgh's lawyer and crime chronicler, William Roughead, into a final battle to clear Slater's name, which, with the valiant aid and oratory of the great advocate, Craigie Aitchison, they succeeded in doing. Despite attempts,

variously respectable, wildly imaginative and downright disreputable, to name the 'real killer', the whole affair remains a complete mystery. Slater died, aged 76, on January 31st, 1948, but his cause goes marching on.

Prime sources: *Notable Scottish Trial,* edited by William Roughead, William Hodge, Edinburgh, 1910.
Revised editions as *Notable British Trial,* 1915, 1925, 1929, 1949.
The Case of Oscar Slater, Arthur Conan Doyle, Hodder & Stoughton, London, 1912.
The Truth About Oscar Slater, William Park, The Psychic Press, London, 1927.
Oscar Slater: The Great Suspect, Peter Hunt, Carroll & Nicholson, London, 1951.

Dr. Thomas Smethurst

Murderer: Dr. Thomas Smethurst.
Victim: Isabella Bankes (bigamous wife) (43).
Locus: 10 Alma Villas, Richmond, Surrey.
Date: May 3rd, 1859.
Means: Irritant poison.
Motive: Financial gain: there was a will in Dr. Smethurst's favour.
Crimewatch: Dr. Smethurst got off. A jury did convict him, but the medical evidence was conflicting and unsatisfactory. The great forensic scientist and toxicologist, Professor Alfred Swaine Taylor, made an error when using the Reinsch test for arsenic in this case which set his own career and the whole of medical jurisprudence back for years. Arsenic was found in an evacuation, but not in Isabella Bankes' body. Small quantities of antimony *were* found in the corpse, but various medicines had been administered. Isabella Bankes was some seven weeks pregnant, and it was argued that she had died of dysentery in pregnancy. Smethurst (aged 54) was reprieved and pardoned. Tried and convicted of bigamy, he was, even so, successful in proving Isabella's will in his favour.

Prime sources: *The Case of Thomas Smethurst, M.D.*, A. Newton, Routledge, Warne, & Routledge, London, 1859. *Notable British Trial,* edited by Leonard A. Parry, William Hodge, Edinburgh, 1931.

George Joseph Smith

The Brides in the Bath Case

Mass Murderer

Murderer: George Joseph Smith.
Victim: Beatrice Constance Annie Mundy (35). Alice Burnham (25). Margaret Elizabeth Lofty (38).
Loci: 80 High Street, Herne Bay, Kent (Mundy). 16 Regent Road, Blackpool (Burnham). 14 Bismarck Road, Highgate Hill, London (Lofty).
Dates: July 13th, 1912 (Mundy). December 12th, 1913 (Burnham). December 18th, 1914 (Lofty).
Means: Drowning in bath.
Motive: Financial gain from life insurance policies and wills.
Crimewatch: Beside the seaside was a fine and private place for G. J. Smith to up-end his brides in the bath. Blue in the face, covered in goose-flesh, poor Bessie Mundy lay surprised, with a piece of Castile soap clutched in her hand. A large lump of hair was left behind in plumpy Alice Burnham's bath. But drowning Margaret Lofty in London was a mistake. The News of the World reported the tragedy, and people made connections. And at the Old Bailey trial for the one murder of Beatrice Mundy, similar fact evidence regarding the other two murders was allowed, by the law that such evidence may be introduced to show a course of conduct. Smith kept interrupting Mr. Justice Scrutton's summing-up. Example: "I am not a murderer, though I may be a bit peculiar." He had a good, Cockney, turn of phrase – 'When they're dead they're dead,' and a sharp line in sarcasm: asked by suspicious relatives to account for himself, he replied, 'My mother was a bus horse, my father a cabdriver, my sister a roughrider over the Arctic

regions. My brothers were all gallant sailors on a steam-roller'. He valued women not at all. After Margaret Lofty's murder, he told his landlady that he was going on a cycling tour. As the same victim wilted newly drowned upstairs, he played on the harmonium in the sitting-room. No evidence that he played "Nearer My Lord to Thee." Born in Bethnal Green, East London, on January 11th, 1872, Smith was hanged at Maidstone Prison on August 13th, 1915.

Prime sources: *Notable British Trial,* edited by Eric R. Watson, William Hodge, Edinburgh, 1922.
George Joseph Smith, Frederick J. Lyons, Duckworth, London, 1935.
The Life and Death of a Ladykiller, Arthur La Berne, Leslie Frewin, London, 1967.

Madeleine Hamilton Smith

Accused: Madeleine Hamilton Smith.
Victim: Pierre Emile L'Angelier (33).
Locus: 7 Blythswood Square, Glasgow.
Date: March 23rd, 1857.
Means: Arsenic.
Motive: Elimination of secret lover no longer desired in order to enter into a convenable marriage.
Crimewatch: Mimi L'Angelier (as she styled herself in her love letters), aged 21, had the benefit of Not Proven. She did pass a cup of cocoa to her importunate lover through the bars of her basement window. This was the hazarded means of administration of arsenic. Madeleine Smith married twice, and died in America on April 12th, 1928, at the age of 93. Buried Mount Hope Cemetery, Westchester, New York, (section 74, Lot 240, Grave 232), as Lena Sheehy.

Prime sources: *Report of the Trial of Madeleine Smith,* Alexander Forbes Irvine, T. & T. Clark, Edinburgh, 1857.
A Complete Report of the Trial of Miss Madeleine Smith, John Morison, William P. Nimmo, Edinburgh, 1857.
The Story of Minie L'Angelier or Madeleine Hamilton Smith, Anonymous, Myles MacPhail, Edinburgh, 1857.
Notable Scottish Trial, edited by A. Duncan Smith, William Hodge, Edinburgh, 1905.
Notable British Trial, edited by F. Tennyson Jesse, William Hodge, Edinburgh, 1927.
The Madeleine Smith Affair, Peter Hunt, Carroll & Nicholson, London, 1950.
That Nice Miss Smith, Nigel Morland, Frederick Muller, London, 1957.

Richard Franklin Speck

Serial killer

Murderer: Richard Franklin Speck.
Victims: Gloria Davy (22). Suzanne Farris (21). Merlita Gargullo (22). Mary Ann Jordan (20). Patricia Matusek (20). Valentina Pasion (23). Nina Schmale (24). Pamela Wilkening (20).
Locus: 2319 East 100th Street, Chicago.
Date: July 14th, 1966.
Means: Strangling and stabbing.
Motive: Sadistic pleasure.
Crimewatch: Tattooed with the presignatory emblem, 'Born to Raise Hell', tall, gangling, pockmarked Speck, born December 6th, 1941, none too bright, obsessive-compulsive, gave a history of repeated head injuries. Electroencephalogram showed no major abnormality. Drink and drugs perhaps more significant. Claimed amnesia for his unparalleled sequence of killings. Entering, armed, a residence for nurses, ostensibly to rob, he tied up nine nurses and led each in turn to another room to slaughter them, at intervals of 20 – 30 minutes. One nurse only, Corazon Amurao, escaped. Only one of his victims, the last, Gloria Davy, was sexually molested. He stripped and sodomized her. She reminded Speck of his estranged wife. His defence, which was run on alibi, not on his mixed psychopathology, failed, and, on June 6th, 1969, he was sentenced to die in the electric chair. Later, his sentence was commuted to a term of 400 to 1,200 years imprisonment at the Stateville Penitentiary, Joliet. He enjoys oil painting.

Prime source: *Born to Raise Hell,* Jack Altman and Martin Ziporyn, M.D., Grove Press, New York, 1967.

Charles Raymond Starkweather

Mass murderer

Murderer: Charles Raymond Starkweather.
Victims: Robert Colvert (21). Marion Bartlett (57).
Velda Bartlett (*c.* 38). Betty Jean Bartlett (2¹/₂).
August Meyer (70). Robert Jensen (17). Carol King
(16). C. Lauer Ward (47). Clara Ward (46). Lillian
Fencl (51). Merle Collison (37).
Loci: Superior Street, a dirt road, just outside
Nebraska City limits (Colvert). 924 Belmont Avenue,
Lincoln (the Bartlett family). Farm 2 miles east of
Bennet, *c.* 20 miles from Lincoln (Meyer). Storm
cellar of demolished schoolhouse near Meyer's farm,
outside Bennet (Jensen, King). 2843 24th Street,
Lincoln (the Wards and Fencl). On Highway 87,
between Casper and Douglas, Wyoming (Collison).
Dates: December 1st, 1957 (Colvert). January 21st,
1958 (the Bartlett family). January 27th, 1958
(Meyer, Jensen, King). January 28th, 1958 (the
Wards and Fencl). January 29th, 1958 (Collison).
Means: Shooting, battering and stabbing.
Motive: Violent expression of hatred of the world,
admixed with convenient acquisition of property by
robbery.
Crimewatch: Born – November 24th, 1938 – on the
wrong side of the Lincoln, Nebraska, tracks,
Starkweather resented his family's low estate.
Sensitivity high, I.Q. 110, small, bow-legged,
unprepossessing, he grew up envious, embittered
and enraged. His job as a garbage-man did not help
his self-esteem. Taking filmic teenage rebel, James
Dean, as his model, he grabbed himself a 14-year-old
girlfriend, Caril Ann Fugate. Starkweather had killed
before – Robert Colvert, of the Crest Service Station,

Cornhusker Highway, just north of Lincoln – for money. He killed Caril's family, the Bartletts, out of hatred. (Caril was the child of a previous marriage.) Then he and his girl went on a three-day murder spree, killing farmer Meyer, Robert Jensen, his fiancée, Carol King, and the millionaire Ward couple and their maid, Lillian Fencl. Travelling shoe-salesman, Merle Collison, was killed for his Buick. Starkweather was arrested, after a car chase, on January 29th, 1958. He and Caril were both charged with murder. Caril, maintaining her innocence, claimed that 'Chuck' had taken her as a hostage on the murder rampage. She was sentenced to life. Paroled 1976. Starkweather died in the electric chair, Nebraska State Penitentiary, shortly after midnight, June 25th, 1959. Asked if he would donate his eyes for transplant after death, he said: 'Hell, no! No one ever did anything for me!'

Prime sources: *The Murderous Trail of Charles Starkweather,* James Melvin Reinhardt, Springfield, Ohio, 1960.
Caril, Ninette Beaver, B. K. Ripley and Patrick Trese, J. B. Lippincott, Philadelphia, 1974.
Starkweather: The Story of a Mass Murderer, William Allen, Houghton Mifflin, Boston, 1976.

152

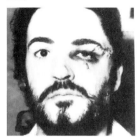

Peter William Sutcliffe

The Yorkshire Ripper

Serial killer

Murderer: Peter William Sutcliffe.
Victims: Wilomena (Wilma) McCann (26 or 28). Emily Monica Jackson (42). Irene Richardson (28). Patricia (Tina) Atkinson (32). Jayne Michelle MacDonald (16). Jean Bernadette Jordan (21). Yvonne Ann Pearson (22). Helen Rytka (18). Vera Millward (41). Josephine Anne Whitaker (19). Barbara Leach (20). Marguerite Walls (47). Jacqueline Hill (20).
Loci: Prince Philip Playing Fields, off Scott Hall Road, Chapeltown, Leeds (McCann). Manor Street, Leeds 7 (Jackson). Soldiers Field, Roundhay, Leeds 8 (Richardson). Flat 3, 9 Oak Avenue, Manningham, Bradford (Atkinson). Adventure Playground between Reginald Terrace and Reginald Street, Chapeltown, Leeds (MacDonald). Land beside Southern Cemetery, Chorlton, Manchester (Jordan). Waste land, Arthington Street, Bradford (Pearson). Garrard's timber yard, Great Northern Street, Huddersfield (Rytka). Car park, Manchester Royal Infirmary (Millward). Savile Park, Bell Hall, Halifax (Whitaker). Ash Grove, Little Horton, Bradford (Leach). Grounds of Claremont House, New Street, Farnsley, Leeds (Walls). Alma Road, Headingley, Leeds (Hill).
Dates: October 30th, 1975 (McCann). January 20th, 1976 (Jackson). February 5th-6th, 1977 (Richardson). April 23rd, 1977 (Atkinson). June 26th, 1977 (MacDonald). October 1st, 1977 (Jordan). January 21st, 1978 (Pearson). January 31st, 1978 (Rytka). May 16th, 1978 (Millward). April 4th, 1979 (Whitaker). September 2nd, 1979 (Leach). August 21st, 1980 (Walls). November 17th, 1980 (Hill).

Means: Swift blows to the head usually with a hammer, often, but not always, of ball-peen type, followed sometimes by strangulation, and attended by deep, eviscerating knife-attack or gouging with a weapon such as a sharpened screwdriver.

Motive: The perverted thrill of killing and despoiling a woman. Not all were prostitutes. Actual sexual contact with the victim was not, usually, a part of the pleasure. The death at his hands was what he wanted, and the slashing at the erogenous zones.

Crimewatch: Sutcliffe – born June 2nd, 1946 – was also convicted of seven similar very severe attempted murders over the 5-year period: Dr. Upaehya Banbara, Marcella Claxton, Maureen Long, Marilyn Moore, Anna Rogulskj, Olive Smelt, Theresa Sykes. At the trial at the Old Bailey in 1981, Mr. Justice Boreham, repudiating plea-bargaining, unexpectedly insisted that a jury should decide if Sutcliffe (who had confessed) was of diminished responsibility by reason of paranoid schizophrenia. Sutcliffe appeared to the team of defence psychiatrists to have experienced a classic 'primary delusion', followed by an 'encapsulated system', when, he claimed, he heard the voice of God at the grave of one Bronislaw Zapolski. But the jury would not accept manslaughter and Sutcliffe was put away in Parkhurst to serve life as a murderer. He might have successfully pleaded Diminished Responsibility by reason of personality disorder, but he was stuck with his 'mission' to kill. Anyway, in March 1984, he was moved to Broadmoor Special Hospital with some form of mental deterioration. And the sinister sender of the faked 'Geordie tapes', which so misled the police, remains at large.

Prime sources: *Deliver Us From Evil,* David A. Yallop, Macdonald Futura, London, 1981.
The Yorkshire Ripper Story, John Beattie, Quartet, London, 1981.
The Yorkshire Ripper, Roger Cross, Granada, London, 1981.
'. . . *somebody's husband, somebody's son',* Gordon Burn, Heinemann, London, 1984.
The Street Cleaner, Nicole Ward Jouve, Marion Boyars, London, 1986.

Arthur Allan Thomas

Accused: Arthur Allan Thomas.
Victims: Jeanette Crewe (30) and her husband, Harvey Crewe (30).
Locus: The Crewe farmhouse, Pukekawa, New Zealand.
Date: June 17th, 1970.
Means: One .22 bullet in the head, in both cases. Jeanette had also received a heavy blow in the face
Motive: Unknown.
Crimewatch: Still a great mystery. Who fed baby Rochelle during the five lost days before the farmhouse behind its screen of macrocarpa trees was discovered bloodstained and empty, except for the small survivor, marooned in her cot? The bodies of both her parents, wrapped in bedding and wire, surfaced separately in the Waikato River in the August and September of 1970. Farmer Arthur Thomas (32), a rejected suitor of Jeanette Crewe, was, in 1971, convicted of double murder, but on December 17th, 1979, he was pardoned and released, endowed with £400,000 compensation. A Royal Commission said that a cartridge case from Thomas' rifle had been put in an area of the Crewes' garden which had previously been pattern-searched and sieved, 'by the hand of one whose duty was to investigate fairly and honestly, but who . . . fabricated this evidence to procure a conviction of murder.'

Prime sources: *Bitter Hill: Arthur Thomas, The Case For a Retrial*, Terry Bell, Avant-Garde Publishing, Manurewa, New Zealand, 1972.
Beyond Reasonable Doubt, David A. Yallop, Hodder & Stoughton, Auckland, New Zealand, 1978.

William Herbert Wallace

Accused: William Herbert Wallace.
Victim: Julia Wallace (52): wife.
Locus: 29 Wolverton Street, Anfield, Liverpool.
Date: January 20th, 1931.
Means: Battering to death.
Motive: None discernible.
Crimewatch: Wallace, insurance agent for the
Prudential, was summoned by a mythical client – Mr.
R. M. Qualtrough – to a non-existent address – 25
Menlove Gardens East, Mossley Hill – by means of a
bogus telephone message to Cottle's City Cafe, in
North John Street, Liverpool, to be delivered to
Wallace when he arrived to play in a chess
tournament later in the evening of Monday, January
19th, 1931. The following evening, returned home
from a fruitless quest, Wallace found his wife brutally
murdered in the parlour. He was arrested, tried,
found guilty and sentenced to death. On appeal the
jury decision was, uniquely, reversed, and Wallace
was liberated. He died, aged 54, of natural causes on
February 26th, 1933. It has since been revealed that
the man whom Wallace himself suspected of having
committed the murder was a former assistant of his
in his insurance work with whom he had had trouble
and who bore him a grudge, Richard Gordon Parry;
and certain circumstances which have been
subsequently attested to strongly suggest that
Wallace, who was almost certainly innocent, was very
likely correct in his suspicions.

Prime sources: *The Trial of William Herbert Wallace,* W. F.
Wyndham-Brown, Gollancz, London, 1933.

The Wallace Case, John Rowland, Carroll & Nicholson, London, 1949.

The Wallace Case, F. J. P. Veale, The Merrymeade Publishing Co. Ltd., Brighton, 1950.

The Killing of Julia Wallace, Jonathan Goodman, Harrap, London, 1969.

Murderer Scot-Free, Robert F. Hussey, David & Charles, Newton Abbot, 1972.

Wallace: The Final Verdict, Roger Wilkes, The Bodley Head, London, 1984.

Kate Webster

Murderer: Kate Webster.
Victim: Julia Martha Thomas.
Locus: 2 Mayfield Villas, Park Road, Richmond, Surrey.
Date: March 2nd, 1879.
Means: According to legend, an attack with an axe.
According to Kate Webster's confession, she threw her
victim down the stairs and then choked her accidentally.
Motive: Financial gain – acquisition of all her mistress'
worldly goods. An element of resentment and
provocation.
Crimewatch: Kate, from Killane, County Wexford, aged
30, quick-tempered, quick-fingered, with 'form' as long
as her sinewy arm, was a fatal choice as a cook-general.
Mrs. Thomas, widowed, alone, in her fifties, was an
epileptic, also quick-tempered, and a notoriously
inconsiderate, carping employer. There were
altercations. Kate was dismissed. But Kate stayed on.
Mrs. Thomas died by her hand on returning from
church, and Kate butchered her remains with a razor, a
meat saw and a carving-knife. Then she boiled the
pieces in the kitchen copper. The head she threw into
the Thames over Hammersmith Bridge, stowed inside a
black American-cloth bag. There was a current legend
that Kate hawked around Richmond two gallopots of
meat dripping rendered down from Mrs Thomas' boiled
body. She fled to Ireland, but the villa was crammed
with clues – charred bones and bloodstains. Tried at the
Old Bailey in July 1879, she
was convicted of wilful murder and hanged at
Wandsworth Prison on July 29th, 1879.

Prime source: *Notable British Trial,* edited by Elliot
O'Donnell, William Hodge, Edinburgh, 1925.

Christopher Bernard Wilder

Serial killer

Murderer: Christopher Bernard Wilder.
Victims: Theresa Ferguson (21). Terry Dianne Walden (23). Suzanne Wendy Logan (21). Beth S. Dodge (33). Missing, no bodies found: Rosario Gonzales (20). Elizabeth Kenyon (23). Sheryl Bonaventure (18). Michelle Korfman (17).
Loci: Disappeared attending Miami Grand Prix motor races (Gonzales). Disappeared from Coral Gables, Florida (Kenyon). Disappeared from shopping mall, Merritt Island, Florida. Body found near Lake Alfred, Florida. (Ferguson). Disappeared from shopping mall, Beaumont, Texas. Body found in canal on outskirts of Beaumont (Walden). Disappeared while shopping in Oklahoma City. Body found on reservoir bank outside Junction City, Kansas (Logan). Disappeared from shopping centre, Grand Junction, Colorado (Bonaventure). Disappeared from shopping mall, Las Vegas, California (Korfman). Corpse discovered in a gravel-pit outside Victor, New York (Dodge).
Dates: The dead: March 18th, 1984 (Ferguson). March 23rd, 1984 (Walden). March 25th, 1984 (Logan). April 12th, 1984 (Dodge). The missing: February 26th, 1984 (Gonzales). March 3rd, 1984 (Kenyon). March 29th, 1984 (Bonaventure). April 1st, 1984 (Korfman).
Means: Beating and stabbing (Ferguson, Walden, Logan). Shooting (Dodge).
Motive: Rape and torture.
Crimewatch: Arrived in Florida from Australia in 1970, the 39-year-old millionaire playboy soon became well known, not only as a race-car driving

ace, but as one of Miami's most eligible bachelors. His wealth, earned from building contracting and invested in real estate, allowed him to indulge a taste for sleek cars, powerful speedboats, luxury homes and stunning playmates. Not bad looking, superbly tailored, renowned animal lover, energetic, amiable, always ready with a smile, Chris seemed to have it all going for him. But he was fatally flawed. He had a hidden, and murderous, cruel streak. He liked to insert an electric prod into his victims and glued one girl's eyelids with Superglue. His tricks had got him arrested for raping two teenage girls in Palm Springs in 1980. He had used a camera as his passport to sexual favours, claiming to be able to turn them into cover girls if they became uncover girls for him. Using the ploy, he went on a trans-America slay ride that left at least eight beautiful girls dead and missing presumed dead. Challenged, on April 13th, 1984, by two New Hampshire state troopers, near Colebrook, pushing the Canada border, he started a scuffle and a bullet from Wilder's own .357 Magnum found its way – either accidentally or suicidally, but lethally – into his heart.

Prime source. *The Beauty Queen Killer,* Bruce Gibney Pinnacle Books, New York, 1984.

Wayne Bertram Williams

The Atlanta Child Murders
Supposed Serial killer

Murderer: Wayne Bertram Williams. Convicted of two murders.
Victims: Jimmy Ray Payne (21). Nathaniel Cater (27).
Locus: Atlanta, Georgia.
Dates: Between April 22nd and April 27th, 1981 (Payne). *c.* May 21st, 1981 (Cater).
Means: Probably asphyxia.
Motive: Presumably sexual gratification.
Crimewatch: Young Blacks kept disappearing in Atlanta. They were mostly male. There were whispers of Ku Klux Klan. In the early hours of May 22nd, 1981, a police recruit in a patrol car on a bridge over the Chattahoochee River heard a splash. Williams, 23 black, an aspiring music entrepreneur, was stopped in his car on the bridge. On May 24th, the body of Nathaniel Cater was found, nude, in the Chattahoochee. At the trial, in 1982, at the Fulton County Courthouse, Williams was tried for only two murders, but evidence relating to ten others was permitted to show 'pattern'. The evidence was circumstantial. There were fibres. The unusually closely-argued Dettlinger/Prugh book made the case disputatious. The fact that the killings ceased on Williams' arrest had been thought to be powerfully evidential, but the Dettlinger study attacks the sanctity of the official list of 28 murders (plus one added by the Prosecution) and names other victims before and after. Williams was sentenced to two consecutive life sentences.
Prime sources: *The List,* Chet Dettlinger with Jeff Prugh, Philmay Enterprises, Atlanta, 1983.
Evidence of Things Not Seen, James Baldwin, Michael Joseph, London, 1986.

Randall Brent Woodfield

Said to be the I-5 Killer
Said to be a serial killer

Murderer: Randall Brent Woodfield.

Victims: Conviction secured only in the one case of Shari Hull (20). Donna Lee Eckard (37) and her daughter, Janell Jarvis (14). Julie Ann Reitz (18).

Loci: TransAmerica Title Building, River Road, Salem, Oregon (Hull). Holiday Road, Mountain Gate, California (Eckard and Jarvis). S. W. Cherryhill Drive, Beaverton, Oregon (Reitz).

Dates: January 18th, 1981 (Hull). February 3rd, 1981 (Eckard and Jarvis). February 15th, 1981 (Reitz).

Means: .32 calibre bullets to the brain (Hull, Eckard, Jarvis). .38 bullet to the brain (Reitz).

Motive: Polymorphous sexual activity, preferably oral, with sodomy.

Crimewatch: Randy Woodfield, born December 26th, 1950, star athlete, drafted for the famous Green Bay Packers football team, was also a chronic indecent exposer, or 'flasher'. Apparently he had felt jealous of his two elder sisters. On one occasion, although he had seemed to be an achiever, his I.Q. tested out as only 100. He had plenty of sexual experience, and herpes, which he passed on to several of his victims. Like Bundy, he favoured a Volkswagen. He often used a .32 silver revolver. As disguise, he stuck Band-Aid over his nose. Up and down the I-5 freeway through California, Oregon and Washington he cruised, raping and robbing, inevitably escalating to random killing. His great mistake was that Julie Reitz was someone he knew. There was strong identification evidence against him, particularly from Beth Wilmot whom he had left for dead, shot beside Shari Hull. There was very strong ballistics evidence, including one rare .32 bullet found in Woodfield's racquetball bag where he lodged at 3622 South E Street, Springfield, Oregon. He was suspected of a number of other unsolved murders. Put away for life plus 125 years in the Oregon State Penitentiary, some of his cases still lying on the books, untried.

Prime source: *The I-5 Killer,* Andy Stack (Ann Rule), Signet Books, New York, 1984.

Graham Frederick Young

Murderer: Graham Frederick Young.

Victims: Molly Young (38): stepmother. Bob Egle (59). Fred Biggs (60).

Loci: 768 North Circular Road, Neasden, West London (Young). Hadland's, Photographic Instrument Firm, Bovingdon, Hertfordshire (Egle, Biggs).

Dates: April 21st, 1962 (Young). July 7th, 1971 (Egle). November 19th, 1971 (Biggs).

Means: Poisoning with thallium.

Motive: Lust for secret power.

Crimewatch: Born September 7th, 1947, at Neasden. Mother died when he was three months old. Giving the impression of being a neat, clean, well behaved, intelligent boy, he was actually obsessed with Hitler, Nazism, black magic, poisons and death. Slow-poisoned his stepmother, Molly Young (38) with antimony and thallium, and attempted to poison his father, Frederick Young (44), sister, Winifred (21) and schoolfriend, Chris Williams (13). Committed to Broadmoor July 1962. Released February 4th, 1971, on the recommendation of Dr. Edgar Udwin. Before leaving told nurse: 'I'm going to kill one person for every year I've spent in this place.' Sent to Government Training Centre at Slough. Poisoned – but not fatally – fellow-trainee storekeeper Trevor Sparkes (34). May 10th, 1971, secured job as storekeeper at John Hadland Ltd., Bovingdon. Shortly after Young's arrival, a spate of mysterious illnesses broke out. They blamed the 'Bovingdon Bug'. Storeroom manager Bob Egle died. So did Fred Biggs, in charge of stocks and distribution. David

Tilson, Jethro Batt (39), Ron Hewitt (41), Peter Buck and Diane Smart (39) were taken ill with varying degrees of severity after drinking tea or coffee provided by Young. Suspicion came to centre on Young. His background was investigated. On November 21st, 1971, he was arrested. In his pocket was a lethal dose of thallium. Tried at St. Albans in July 1972, he told the warders that if convicted he would break his own neck on the dock rail. He died in Parkhurst Prison after a heart attack on August 1st, 1990, aged 42.

Prime sources: *Obsessive Poisoner,* Winifred Young, Robert Hale, London, 1973.
The St. Albans Poisoner, Anthony Holden, Hodder & Stoughton, London, 1974.

INDEX